Digital Rise: The Journey of AI, VR, and XR

Expanded Version

John V. Campanella

Contents

To Dana,
For your endless love, support, and inspiration, this book is lovingly
dedicated to you.
With all my heart,

John

Preface

The Journey of AI, VR, and XR into the Future

Volume 2: Expanded Version

In the "Digital Rise" book series, we embark on an explorative journey through the evolving landscapes of Digital Technologies including Artificial Intelligence (AI), Virtual Reality (VR), and Extended Reality (XR). This first book, "The Journey of AI, VR, and XR," we chronicle the rise, development, and future trajectory of these groundbreaking technologies, which have become the keystones of the digital revolution reshaping our world.

The story of AI begins with the dream of creating machines capable of human-like thought and reasoning. We trace this journey from its theoretical roots, through the era of early computing, and into today's world, where AI influences everything from healthcare and finance to our daily interactions with smart devices. The narrative delves into the milestones that have marked AI's progress, the winters it has endured, and the renaissance it experiences today.

Simultaneously, we explore the realm of VR, a technology that has transcended its science-fiction origins to become a conduit to worlds as vast as our imagination. "Digital Rise" examines VR's metamorphosis from its early prototypes to the sophisticated systems that now provide immersive experiences in gaming, education, and therapy. We witness VR's power to transport us to new realities, offering experiences that challenge our perceptions of the virtual and the real.

The journey then expands into the domain of XR, where the physical and digital worlds converge. This section of the book looks at the spectrum of technologies, from AR to MR, showcasing how they blend the real with the digital. We explore XR's applications in various industries, its role in enhancing human interaction, and its potential to redefine experiential learning and collaboration.

As we navigate through the histories and current states of AI, VR, and XR, "Digital Rise" also projects into their futures. We discuss emerging trends, potential challenges, and the evolving frontiers of these technologies. The book addresses the societal, ethical, and philosophical questions they raise, contemplating the future they are shaping—a future where digital and physical realities are increasingly intertwined.

The "Digital Rise" series is crafted for a diverse audience, from tech enthusiasts and industry professionals to students and general readers curious about the digital transformation of our world. Through comprehensive analysis, expert insights, and forward-looking predictions, we provide a panoramic view of where we are and where we are heading in the digital realm.

Join us on this enlightening journey through the annals of technology, where we explore the rise of digital worlds and the convergence of realities. "Digital Rise: The Journey of AI, VR, and XR" is not just a story of technological advancement; it is a narrative about the human spirit's relentless pursuit of innovation and the reshaping of our existence in the digital age.

Chapter One

The Dream of Intelligent Machines

Ancient Myths and Automata

The idea of artificial beings coming to life has fascinated people since ancient times. Greek mythology contains many such stories that illustrate early ideas about artificial life. The tale of the sculptor Pygmalion, who carved a woman out of ivory so beautiful that he fell in love with his creation, is one of the most famous. After praying to Aphrodite, the goddess of love, Pygmalion returned home to find that his sculpture had come to life as Galatea.

Another key figure in Greek mythology was Hephaestus, the god of blacksmiths, craftsmen, and artisans. Often depicted in his forge creating intricate mechanical devices, Hephaestus made golden servant girls to help him in his work. The idea that an artificial being could demonstrate agency and assist humans with tasks foreshadowed concepts central to AI.

Ancient China and Egypt also incorporated ideas of mechanical servants and self-operating devices. The legendary Chinese inventor Yan Shi created a humanoid automaton that could sing and dance. In ancient Egypt, statues of deities were sometimes rigged with systems of ropes, and priests controlled them to perform rituals, move, and speak to followers. Across early civilizations, the drive to imbue mechanical creations with life-like qualities persisted as a common thread.

Al-Jazari and the Islamic Golden Age

The early 13th century marked the Islamic Golden Age, a period of scientific advancement, economic development, and cultural flourishing. A key figure was the Arab polymath Al-Jazari, who made groundbreaking contributions to mechanical engineering. He served the Artuqid kings of Diyar-Bakr in modern Turkey as chief engineer and devised water-raising machines, water clocks, and intricate automata.

In 1206 CE, al-Jazari completed his book "The Book of Knowledge of Ingenious Mechanical Devices," documenting his designs. This treatise described over 50 mechanical devices and automata, including automatic doors, musical robots powered by water, and a waitress that could serve drinks. The creativity and complexity of these creations placed al-Jazari as a pioneer in the field of robotics centuries before the term was coined. The influence of his automatic machines on the development of mechanized robots is impossible to overstate.

The Renaissance and The Age of Enlightenment

The Renaissance period spanning 14th to 17th century Europe saw an explosion of interest in the scientific method and classical learning. As a result of humanist ideologies that emphasized respect for human dignity and individual ability, inventors turned back to mechanical automation, which blurred the lines between art and technology.

Leonardo da Vinci exemplified the Renaissance spirit through his study of anatomy, nature, art, and his designs for machines like self-propelled carts and proto-calculators. He drew designs for a pulley- and cable-powered humanoid automaton that could sit up, wave its arms, and move its head using a flexible neck mechanism. While seemingly far ahead of its time, da Vinci's imagined robot embodied the era's spirit of using science and art to mimic life.

The Enlightenment era of the 17th and 18th centuries featured prominent thinkers laying the foundations of modern philosophy, science, and mathematics. Influential rationalists such as René Descartes and Gottfried Wilhelm Leibniz made significant contributions pertinent to AI. In his 1637 Discourse on Method, Descartes advanced a mechanical view of biology, described reflex actions, and proposed that the bodies of humans and animals function akin to machines.

In his 1714 Monadology theoretical treatise, Leibniz hypothesized that all things in nature are comprised of indivisible substances and have "perception" and "appetites" driving their actions. He went further to imagine that man could invent artificial mechanisms with perceptions similar to those found in nature. Though rudimentary, these perspectives foreshadowed critical debates about machine versus biological intelligence.

The Industrial Revolution and Automata

The Industrial Revolution, beginning in the late 18th century, radically transformed manufacturing through mechanization. Steam power drove mechanical automation, allowing mass production of goods previously made by hand. This capacity for precise, repetitive fabrication at scale powered demand for automatons—machines that simulated humans and animals.

Inventors across Europe produced all manner of self-operating mechanical devices, blurring the line between machine and living being. Jacques de Vaucanson gained fame for his digesting duck automaton, which featured over 1000 moving parts that could flap wings, eat grain, and defecate. Henri Maillardet created an automaton that could draw four images and write three poems. These lifelike qualities in truly advanced automata fascinated the public and drew conversations about the replication of life toward fruitful philosophical directions.

The undisputed popularity peak for automata came in the form of Wolfgang von Kempelen's chess playing "Turk" hoax. Unveiled in 1770, this fake automaton masted by a hidden human chess master to defeat opponents deceived onlookers for decades. While later revealed to be an illusion, the Turk exploited the public image of automata as thinking, rational machines. The spectacle thrust concepts of mechanical intelligence into mainstream debate and popular culture for the first time.

Early 20th Century Science Fiction

By the early 1900s, rapid progress in mechanization and factory automation set the stage for more complex conjectures around intelligent machines. Fiction writers began exploring primordial questions of technological creationism through a scientific lens.

In his 1920 play R.U.R. (Rossum's Universal Robots), Czech writer Karel Čapek coined the term "robot." His play features Rossum's Universal Robots—synthetic people made of flesh and blood. Though organic, these beings exhibit free thought and turn on their human masters, illustrating some of the first tensions between creator and creation in robotic science fiction.

No writer influenced robot ethics more than Isaac Asimov, whose short story collection I, Robot, published in 1950, introduced the "Three Laws of Robotics." These precepts state that robots cannot harm humans, must obey orders, and must protect themselves unless these actions conflict with the first two laws. Asimov's simple tenets highlighted complex moral questions when dealing with intelligent machines.

Other sci-fi works emphasized the risks of technological invention, most famously Mary Shelley's Frankenstein or the Modern Prometheus, originally published in 1818. Drawing on the Greek tale of Prometheus creating man, Shelley's scientist Victor Frankenstein manufactures a hideous creature from corpses, which eventually destroys him. This theme of creation beyond human control and its unintended ruinous consequences echoed across modern science fiction, infusing the public imagination around AI with notes of apprehension.

Mathematical Foundations

Alongside the evolution of cultural myths and fictional narratives, the 20th century bore witness to pivotal formal milestones in computation and algorithmic learning, seminal to artificial intelligence.

In his 1936 paper "On Computable Numbers," British mathematician Alan Turing formulated the theoretical basis for computer computation. He proposed an abstract machine consisting of a limitless tape of symbols, a read-write head, and a table of symbol manipulation instructions. These "Turing machines" set the limits of mechanical computation and proved fundamental for the later digital computer.

Turing also devised the famous Turing test as a measure of machine intelligence. The test requires a human evaluator to communicate with both a machine and a human respondent via text interface. The machine passes if the evaluator cannot reliably distinguish between it and the human respondent after several interactions. While criticized as an inadequate intelligence metric, the underlying concept proved hugely influential in AI progress.

In tandem, American mathematician Alonzo Church wrote a paper introducing Lambda calculus, which allows computation through symbolic equation manipulation. Church and Turing later showed that Lambda calculus and Turing machines both formed equivalent universal systems describing the same computational processes. These connections make theories of computation indispensable to cultivating AI.

Later, mathematician John Von Neumann proposed the computer architecture still used today. His 1945 First Draft of a Report on the EDVAC outlined the logical design of a stored-program computer comprising processor, memory, mass storage, and input/output modules. This robust theoretical scaffold enabled the first practical electronic computers critical to realizing artificial intelligence aims.

Conclusion

Over the years, AI's rich history has created a complex web of ideas that include fantastical stories about false life and human arrogance, clever but limited mechanical automata, thought-provoking scientific experiments, classic science fiction tropes, and formal theories that are at the heart of modern computing. These diverse historical threads stitch together a motley tapestry upon which the origins of artificial intelligence are set. From this foundation of creative scientific curiosity and experimentation, present-day AI emerged as technology finally caught up with imagination. Just as fictional concepts materialized into reality, today's machines are transcending perceived limitations toward attaining their own flavor of intelligence. What new fruits will this union yet bear as AI continues maturing through the coming century?

Chapter Two

Alan Turing

The Visionary

Alan Turing: Pioneer of Computing and Artificial Intelligence

A lan Turing was one of the most influential scientists and mathematicians of the 20th century. Often regarded as the "father of computer science and artificial intelligence," Turing made groundbreaking contributions that fundamentally advanced computing and laid the theoretical substrate for the eventual realization of AI.

The Concept of the Turing Machine

Perhaps Turing's most renowned contribution stems from his 1936 paper, "On Computable Numbers, with an Application to the Entscheidungsproblem" where he outlined the idea of a Turing machine. The Turing machine is a conceptual device that forms the very basis for what can be computed mechanically.

In its abstract form, a Turing machine consists of an infinitely long tape marked out in cells each containing a symbol, a read-write head that scans each cell and detects the symbol within, and a table of transition rules. Based on the scanned symbol and its internal state, the Turing machine can then carry out certain actions, such as writing a new symbol, moving the tape left or right, or transitioning to a different internal state as per its transition table guidelines.

Despite its simple design, Turing demonstrated how this conceptual machine could theoretically perform any mechanical computational task, provided it is able to complete in finite time. The Turing machine could replicate the logic behind any algorithmic process by changing states and modifying symbols systematically based on predetermined rules.

Turing further showed mathematically that there exists a Universal Turing Machine that, given the right encoding of any specific Turing machine's description and transition table as input data, can simulate the logic of that particular Turing machine. This crucial concept of a general-purpose machine formed the keystone for the idea of programmable computers.

The paper had a monumental impact on both computer science and mathematics. It established fundamental restrictions on the types of problems that computational processes can solve—the halting problem equivalent. Additionally, it proved that it is impossible to determine whether a statement in a formal mathematical system is provable, which was a long-standing issue that mathematician David Hilbert raised in 1928.

The Turing Test for Machine Intelligence

A later seminal publication by Turing in 1950 titled "Computing Machinery and Intelligence" framed the enduring question, "Can machines think?" Here, he replaced this vague problem with a more concrete behavioral approach.

Turing proposed an "imitation game" in which a human interrogator communicates with two entities—another human and a machine—and must determine, based on conversational responses, which is which. If the machine can consistently convince evaluators over extended discourse that it is human, it passes the test.

This paradigm, universally known today as "the Turing Test," shifts focus from vaguely defining "thinking" to observable evidence of human-machine intelligence parity via verbal behavior. It provides an empirical assessment grounded in people's lived understanding of human intellectual abilities. The test also circumvents the need to precisely define the nebulous concept of "intelligence" itself.

The Turing Test has provoked both enthusiastic support and criticism regarding its validity as a metric for evaluating progress in AI abilities relative to humans. Nonetheless, it strongly directed attention to natural language processing and interactivity as key frontiers in developing systems that can engage in sophisticated, meaningful dialogue on equal terms as people. This orientation guiding AI ambitions persists today.

Turing and the Wartime Bombe

Turing's contributions extend far beyond theoretical horizons to active real-world systems engineering. During World War II, Turing worked as part of the British cryptanalytic team at Bletchley Park attempting to decipher encrypted communications from the German Enigma machines. These cipher devices allowed the German military to securely encode strategic messages using billions of permutations.

Here, Turing designed the electromechanical Bombe device aimed at methodically breaking Enigma codes. Imitating parts of the Enigma machine's logic, the Bombe helped detect rotor wirings within the Enigma setup by systematically guessing settings and ruling out logical inconsistencies. This regulation enabled the Bombe to zero in on the original configuration used to encode each message.

The advent of high-speed Bombes effectively mechanized and accelerated much of the cryptanalytic attack, allowing the Allies to reliably decipher critical German communications throughout the war. Historical assessments credit this decisive information edge in significantly advancing the Allied victory. Turing's brilliant interdisciplinary engineering, considering both mathematical logic and physical machinery, was instrumental to this end.

Post-War Computing and Legacy

After the war, Turing continued advancing the computer science frontiers both theoretically and practically. He articulated foundational ideas like neural networks and genetic algorithms, uncannily presaging machine learning decades prior to its realization. Turing also worked on early computer engineering projects like the ACE (Automatic Computing Engine) and Manchester Mark 1 digital computers, among the world's first stored-program electronic computers.

Turing's philosophical spirit permeating his contributions is summarized in poignant quotes. On the destiny of advancing intelligence, Turing observed, "We can only see a short distance ahead, but we can see plenty there that needs to be done." Regarding the inverse Turing Test he formulated, "A computer would deserve to be called intelligent if it could deceive a human into believing that it was human." This guiding criterion endures as a central touchstone in AI milestones.

In retrospection, Turing's influence reigns among the most fertile founding fathers of computer science and AI. The Turing machine established the abstraction delineating computable functions to model computer programs mechanically. The Turing Test qualitatively ranked intelligent ability based on indistinguishability from human conversation. And the Enigma-breaking Bombe conjunto mechanized the technique of systematic logic deconstruction that later crystallized into automated learning algorithms.

Each contribution formed both a philosophical framework and an engineering breakpoint, propelling technology toward modern digitization and intelligent automation. Seven decades later, the present Cambrian explosion of computing power, data scale and algorithmic accessibility can trace its conceptual seeds back to Turing's visions, which at the time verged on science fiction. Today, Turing's once fantastical dreams manifest incrementally.

Chapter Three

John McCarthy

The Birth of AI

The Dartmouth Conference: The Birthplace of Artificial Intelligence

The summer of 1956 marked an seminal point in the history of technology when the field of Artificial Intelligence formally crystallized during an intensive 8-week workshop at Dartmouth College. Convened by a small group of pioneering researchers, this exploratory incubator delivered the concept of "Artificial Intelligence" itself while forging connections between luminaries that redirected the landscape of automated reasoning for decades to follow.

The Spark of Imagination

The Dartmouth Conference traced its origins to a radical idea seeded in the mind of one ambitious scientist, John McCarthy. In 1955, McCarthy was an assistant professor of mathematics at Dartmouth, lecturing on computational complexity theory. A veteran of the Manhattan Project, McCarthy sought to extend automated computation from numerical calculation to higher-order logic and symbolic abstraction.

During a bus commute, McCarthy was gazing out the window while pondering a hypothetical question: could complex human analytical tasks be defined unambiguously enough for a machine to execute them? In a flash of insight, he conceived of organizing a collaborative research effort focused specifically on exploring this possibility in depth. McCarthy took the first step by writing a proposal drafted with colleague Claude Shannon and distributing it among eminent researchers for feedback.

This document laid out the visionary hypothesis that "every aspect of learning or any other feature of intelligence can in principle be so precisely described that a machine can be made to simulate it." The proposal ambitiously called for convening a meeting of experts across mathematics, computer science, psychology and neuroscience, among other disciplines, at Dartmouth College in the summer of 1956. This forum aimed to crystallize the common unifying interest among these fields into a concrete research agenda and formalize a new field investigating the prospect of replicating human intellectual abilities through artificial means—hence the term "Artificial Intelligence."

The Gathering at Dartmouth

The resulting workshop managed to attract a 10-person delegation of foremost thinkers to the idyllic college campus for a freewheeling incubation of ideas. Attendees included pioneers such as computer scientist Marvin Minsky, cognitive psychologist Allen Newell, alongside colleague Herbert Simon, who devised the Logic Theorist algorithm, Nathaniel Rochester, who directed the IBM effort toward intelligent automation, and Claude Shannon, the father of information theory.

The informal schedule facilitated rapid fire exchanges exploring everything from neurological models to philosophical definitions of abstraction. There were intimate blackboard jam sessions more reminiscent of academic dorm lounges than typical technical conferences. Participants jumped between pondering human cognition and problem solving using the latest software tools and computing systems brought onsite by the IBM team.

The interdisciplinary discourse forged connections between previously disconnected advocates groping at the edges of automated reasoning: the mathematician's programmable logic, the engineer's instinct toward mechanism, and the psychologist's approximations of human thought. A collective identity coalesced. The term "Artificial Intelligence" itself consciously selected by McCarthy did much to conceptually orient what had largely existed as disparate threads pursuing machine-based analysis.

Outcomes: Software Synthesis and Lasting Partnerships

In later years, the Dartmouth Conference came to be recognized as the official birthplace of AI research, yet its direct tangible yield was initially quite modest. The meeting produced no landmark papers or groundbreaking prototypes. Its significance lay more in strengthening personal cooperation and cross-pollination between brilliant visitors already wrestling with core concepts embryonic to AI.

The most immediate byproduct was to deepen partnerships that later built pioneering systems fundamental to AI's unfolding chronology. Newell and Simon leveraged Dartmouth's energy upon returning to Carnegie Mellon University directly to create the Logic Theorist software, one of the world's first examples of non-numeric algorithmic problem solving coded for a computer. This program managed to automatically derive proofs for many challenging theorems from Whitehead and Russell's Principia Mathematica using symbolic manipulation, an impressive display of machine reasoning.

McCarthy himself took up a professorship at MIT shortly after the workshop to launch the AI Group and oversee the creation of Lisp, a programming language tailored for processing symbolic representations of knowledge. Minsky later joined forces with McCarthy before splitting off to found MIT's own AI laboratory, advancing neural network approaches. In effect, Dartmouth spawned a generation of expandable facilities, earnestly pursuing the fruits of automated intellect for decades.

Ever-Shifting Goalposts: From Amazing to Ambient

The cultural fallout from Dartmouth also profoundly redirected mindsets around capabilities commonly ascribed to human exclusivity. Natural language understanding, game strategy, artistic creativity, social interplay and common sense logic joined arithmetic calculation, data retrieval and rote task handling on the manifest of machine modes predicted to inevitably fall under algorithmic control.

Promises now routine, like smartphone assistants, movie recommendation engines and automatic photo tagging, were Jetsonian fantasies brought somewhat into substance after Dartmouth initialized the organized assault upon AI's barriers. Each hard-won software breakthrough around game complexity, phonetic parsing or contextual relevance cracked formerly solid assumptions about computers being rigid rule-based contraptions unable to handle open-ended inference.

Yet despite the ground gained by AI implementations, the goal posts distinguishing routine functions from advanced intelligence continue shifting further away as apparently clever technologies are subsumed into the fabric of the everyday. Minsky himself wryly observed this phenomenon, noting that "as soon as it works, no one calls it AI anymore." The paradoxical consequence of AI's advances steadily assimilating into ambient convenience is the perpetually receding horizon where machines remain obviously inept, in contrast to human talents constantly taken for granted. Perhaps the ultimate triumph possible for AI lies not in matching people but rather in rendering technology itself invisible through effective design, dissolving arbitrary divisions between nature and artifice.

Historical Import: Invigorating Interdisciplinary Insight

The Dartmouth Conference occupies a seminal position in technology history analogous to the big bang creation moment setting the field's expansion in motion. By formally baptizing research toward mimicking intelligence as a unified endeavor called "AI," Dartmouth crystallized disparate visions into a declared science. It connected pioneers guided more by raw creativity than established principles. And it indelibly set loose autonomous intellect from sole human custody where no bank of machinery had previously threatened to trespass.

At one point, McCarthy emphasized the obligation toward enriching factual grounding in such exploratory excursions by observing, "He who refuses to do arithmetic is doomed to talk nonsense." This sentiment captured the integral role mathematical rigor plays in evolving aspirational guesswork into reliable technology. The wizardry summoned through today's machine learning formulas arguably traces directly back to McCarthy's primitive algebraic musings on a bus back in 1955, dreaming about definitive rule systems to emulate thinking.

Now, seven decades hence, as once untouchable milestones like chess mastery, medical diagnosis and creative composition blink under the specter of algorithms, McCarthy's proposal to align our brightest minds in a common journey seems visionary. And while the original goal of encoding any singular formal model to recreate general intelligence remains elusive, the collective progress bridging the divides between code and cognition continues to open new passages of understanding. In many ways, the lasting bequest of the inaugural AI gathering at Dartmouth lies not in any immediate breakthrough invention but rather in the interdisciplinary community it summoned together. This constitution set the course toward reconciling the timeless mysteries of human reason alongside computable mechanisms rapidly reshaping reality.

Chapter Four

Early AI Systems

Pioneering Programs: The Logic Theorist, ELIZA and the Advent of Artificial Intelligence

The earliest inklings of artificial intelligence emerged through pioneering software architectures constructed in the domains of logical reasoning and natural language processing. Two seminal programs called the Logic Theorist and ELIZA surfaced between 1955 and 1966, demonstrating computers' capacity to replicate signature aspects of human intellect: mathematical proof derivation and conversational dialogue. These prototypes have rich potential for cultivating artificial thinking machines.

The Logic Theorist: Automating the Process of Deduction

One foundation stone heralding AI came as a proof-solving algorithm named the Logic Theorist, developed in 1955 by Allen Newell, Herbert Simon and Cliff Shaw at the RAND Corporation think tank. Simon and Newell were both cognitive psychologists interested in modeling the mechanisms of human problem-solving. They identified elementary logic—the symbolic reasoning underpinning fields from computer science to moral philosophy—as fertile ground for constructing an explicit set of heuristics an automated system could follow to mimic deduction. This core insight birthed the Logic Theorist software.

The program operated within the framework of mathematical logic that Alfred North Whitehead and Bertrand Russell laid out in their seminal Principia Mathematica volumes. This system codified the branch of mathematics centered on systematic deduction using axioms and inferential rules rather than numeric computation. Using this framework, Newell and Simon devised a program architecture encompassing three key components.

First, a memory stores definitions for primitive logical operators like AND, OR, and NOT alongside axioms and already proven theorems. Second, a simulator used these elements to incrementally generate new propositions and implications. And third, a rule set encoded valid inferential steps that could extend existing proofs toward some target thesis based on substitution, detachment and other classical techniques.

This design allowed for the development of extended sequences of inference rooted in basic axioms while preserving overall validity at each derivation. By governing the logical system, the program thereby produced chains demonstrating mathematical truths purely by symbolic artificial reasoning.

The Logic Theorist successfully managed proofs for 38 of the 52 Principia theorems attempted, comparable in outcome to skilled humans working through the same problems manually at the time. One output even uncovered a more elegant proof than what Russell originally devised by hand. Newell and Simon's results published in 1956 galvanized many to recognize computing potential extending beyond mere number crunching into sophisticated cognition like logical deduction, formerly deemed too abstract for machines.

The logic theorist fulfilled a dual role, both as a standalone technical achievement and a harbinger of far deeper horizons in computers processing connective symbolic reasoning similar to people. At once a prototype expert system representing structured human knowledge and also existence proof that key elements of intellect operate formulaically enough to yield before coded, automated formulation. Thereby set in motion greater aspirations toward general thinking machines.

ELIZA: A Natural Language Conversing Companion

Another illuminating application named ELIZA emerged from MIT around 1964, standing upon the Logic Theorist's initial steps toward higher-order information processing goals. ELIZA was coded by computer scientist Joseph Weizenbaum to demonstrate computers navigating another mode of cognition long considered too ambiguous for programming: fluid human conversation.

Weizenbaum created ELIZA to operate as an artificial mock psychotherapist, conversing in natural language with users about their emotional lives and personal worries. It modeled the Rogerian technique of reflecting patient statements back as open-ended questions to encourage deeper disclosure. The aim was to create the illusion of empathetic dialogue without any actual understanding.

Mechanically, ELIZA employed pattern matching and substitution methodology to analyze user input for emotional keywords, which it would then repackage into customized phrases, promoting further interaction. If one typed "I'm worried my kids are ungrateful," ELIZA might return, "Why does that make you worried about your children?" selectively pulling terms while ignoring syntactic coherence. It managed reasonable exchanges within narrow bounds before eventually becoming repetitive.

Nonetheless, ELIZA proved disarmingly successful as an interactive conversational agent, even in its primitive 1960s implementation. Many test subjects were startled upon realizing the exchange lacked any computerized representation of meanings, assuming instead they were conversing with a human. Alongside demonstrating computers' expanding linguistic faculties, it surfaced provocative questions about emotional connection, perhaps reducible to formulaic verbal rituals.

Weizenbaum himself grew troubled observing ELIZA's plausibly therapeutic effects despite hollow insides, making evident how readily people project humanity onto systems, merely reconfiguring their own words back at them. This tendency for speculative mythologizing around embryonic thinking technologies highlighted psychological undercurrents latent in AI ambitions.

The ELIZA software likewise sets an agenda around language interfaces, understanding context and social relationships as integral frontiers for cultivating intuitive machine intelligence on par with animal or anthropic capabilities taken for granted. Its lasting imprint remains in conception rather than direct technological progeny. Yet anchoring intelligence in conversational ability continues to shape assessments around progress in humanized artificial reasoning.

Lasting Relevance: Proof by Prototype

Together, the Logic Theorist and ELIZA composed a conceptual couplet, incarnating ideas of automated expertise in dual domains of logic and language central to sapient inference. Each program concretized hypotheses about formalizing conditions sufficient to computerize particular modes of abstract thought. At the same time, both systems set philosophical trajectories, and popular consciousness around cybernetic intelligence rapidly departed from the merely mechanical.

These pioneering programs also surfaced timeless themes in AI that are still resurgent today. The contrast between solving narrowly defined problems efficiently versus addressing general tasks in an open world. How system behaviors shape perceptions of internal capabilities goes beyond the actual mechanisms. The tendency to underestimate subtle faculties integral to human thinking that evade capture through purely logical specification. And embodiment factors involving identity, emotion, and culture transcend pure information processing challenges.

Both projects' symbolic methods sank swiftly under the algorithmic wave of statistical machine learning decades later. Yet their success in demonstrating principles separated them from crude derivatives of human control systems that merely enacted complex input-output mappings. In framing cognition itself through an algorithmic lens, these programs rendered ambient intellectual feats accessible by artificial design. Thereby, the Logic Theorist and ELIZA ventured significant steps enroute to intelligible machines.

The Quest for AI Underway

In 1957, Simon publicly predicted that machines would achieve universal human cognitive abilities within 10 years. This dramatic overreach belies the depth remaining in modeling even narrowly intelligent competencies. Yet progress continues incrementally cascading across once impregnable capabilities making the incremental climb toward more expansive artificially intelligent systems.

Today, logical reasoning routines enabled by these conceptual pioneers channel massive computational power into advanced applications like financial portfolio management, contract analytics and scientific discovery support. Meanwhile, conversational interfaces from simple rule-based chatbots to context-aware voice agents provide everyday assistance to millions, granting a flavor of the human-machine dialogue Weizenbaum envisioned.

And new hybrid techniques further close divides between fluid social intelligence and structured problem solving. The integrated reasoning behind apps like visual search, language translation and robotic environmental navigation rely upon fusing logical representation with statistical learning. Extending these mergers toward more flexible human-like cognition remains an open grand challenge.

The initial sparks toward machine reasoning struck from humble software seeds like the Logic Theorist and ELIZA now cascade into a vast interdisciplinary mission drawing global investment, data and talent aiming squarely at realizing artificial general intelligence surpassing human performance. Yet core questions and themes aired within these pioneering programs' constrained architectures continue casting relevance, caution and inspiration over the winding route ahead. Their legacy echoes through each incremental climb toward artificial brains possessing both logical precision and ambiguity tolerant wisdom.

Chapter Five

AI Gains Momentum

The Development of Machine Learning

The Odyssey of Machine Learning: From Neural Networks to Deep Learning and Beyond

The quest to create intelligent machines has captured human imagination for centuries. This pursuit found its most promising expression in the field of machine learning, empowering computers to learn and improve at tasks independently. The evolution of machine learning algorithms over the past seven decades has interweaved pioneering visions, conceptual setbacks, resurgent ideas and high-performance implementations detonating across industries.

The journey continues today through rising techniques like deep reinforcement learning, GPU-acceleration and transfer learning applied to everything from protein folding predictions to autonomous robo-taxis. This odyssey of machine learning chronicles pivotal milestones, outstanding challenges and horizons yet unfathomed.

The Early Neural Network Visionaries

The foundational concepts underpinning machine learning date back to the early days of computer science itself. As early as the 1940s, pioneers like Walter Pitts and Warren McCulloch explored simplified mathematical models for biological neural processing. These early models represented neural activity through threshold activation functions and formed logic gates analogous to digital circuits.

In 1958, Frank Rosenblatt built upon this groundwork to design the Perceptron, one of the first machine learning algorithms for pattern recognition. Perceptron's simulated nerves are adjustable connections between input and output neuron layers. Binary threshold activations determine firing, similar to spiking neurons. By incrementally tuning synapse weights, perceptron's "learned" how to cluster input data, such as images, into shape categories.

This architecture foreshadowed entire classes of feedforward neural networks, including multilayer perceptron's and convolutional neural networks dominating computer vision today. Yet limitations around linear separability hampered more expansive adoption. Even though they got a lot of attention at first, perceptron's did not really make a difference in machine learning because there was not a good way to send errors back to the layers that do the tuning. Instead, they were just interesting to look at.

Setback and Recovery Through Backpropagation

Interest in machine learning entered a fallow period through the 1970s as limitations accumulated regarding the scalability of prevailing techniques. The inability for shallow neural networks to solve complex nonlinear problems reduced the appetite for funding. Overinflated hype around embryonic algorithms also jaded enthusiasm. This retrenchment denoted the first "AI Winter"—a cycle recurring as inflated expectations repeatedly outpaced implementations.

Innovations revitalizing machine learning emerged in the mid-1980s by rehabilitating concepts from past pioneers. Building on a principle posited years earlier in 1974 by Paul Werbos, Geoffrey Hinton's research team introduced generalizable error backpropagation, facilitating the tuning of multilayer networks. By quantifying derivates of error with respect to any weights across internal network layers, backpropagation enabled the modeling of intricately nonlinear functions via neural networks through chained partial differentiation.

This breakthrough fueled a renaissance in neural networks, ushering architectures such as long short-term memory (LSTMs) recurrent neural networks able to connect previous context with present input. Suddenly, model complexity could scale to the data rather than vice versa. As available datasets grew exponentially in the 1990s due to increased computing capacity alongside the internet's inflation of information, backpropagation became the fulcrum to hoist a new machine learning epoch.

Statistical Learning and Support Vector Machines

Alongside neural networks, a parallel machine learning tradition sprang from algorithmic inference on probabilistic models for prediction and analysis. This approach focused on mathematically minimizing expected error to make reliable generalizations from finite samples. Researchers sought to formalize principles determining how systems could most effectively extract insights from data itself as opposed to relying purely on hard-coded rules.

Key developments in the 1990s included Vladimir Vapnik's advances in distilling support vector machines (SVMs) for classification and regression using convex optimization. By identifying marginal boundaries maximally separating groups of points, SVMs could categorize new data with low error in line with computational learning theory. As neural networks and statistical learning merged into mutually reinforced hybrids, the field coalesced toward what is recognized as modern machine learning today.

The Cambrian Explosion of Deep Learning

The accumulating breakthroughs in managing model complexity, algorithm optimization and parallel computing over these decades primed machine learning for a vertical explosion in efficacy once key remaining limitations were unlocked. In the 2010s, this change happened when all the previous progress was put together into deep neural network architectures made up of many processing layers that work together according to algorithms.

Hardware innovations, particularly general-purpose graphical processing units (GPUs) capable of massively parallel floating-point calculations, delivered raw firepower to optimize much larger models. Large categorized datasets, such as the ImageNet image library, containing over 15 million annotated samples, provided supervised training targets. Together, these conditions propelled breakthroughs, manifesting orders of magnitude in performance leaps.

In a 2012 ImageNet computer vision competition, a convolutional neural network called AlexNet achieved over 15% higher accuracy than the next best entry. The deep learning epitomized in AlexNet soon revolutionized fields from speech recognition to machine translation, seemingly overnight, through the dominance of benchmark challenges. Its proficiency continues to expand applications, including drug design, self-driving vehicles, content generation and beyond, by exploiting relationships within colossal volumes of data unavailable to lone researchers.

Persistent Challenges and Future Horizons

Today, machine learning has evolved from its crude neurological origins into an accelerated scientific juggernaut, fueling paradigm shifts in how humanity leverages information. Yet fundamental conceptual gaps persist despite mounting tactical successes. Contemporary models optimized for narrowly defined tasks rarely transfer cleanly to even modestly different domains or data distributions without substantial retraining. Shutting systems down logically for debugging or maintenance frequently breaks learned behaviors lacking modular internal reasoning.

And opaque bulk processing obfuscates interpretability into these AI black boxes, such that the causes underlying their states or decisions remain mysterious to direct inspection. Solving these structural knowledge gaps separating machine learning from higher-order cognition likely demands revisiting symbolic logical mechanisms layered atop distributed numerical processing. Hybrid neuro-symbolic architectures strike toward this future, delivering adaptable, interpretable and stable intelligent systems enriched by underlying structural awareness and causal understanding augmented through learned empirical associations.

Reinforcement learning, few-shot learning and adversarial training carry momentum as well in overcoming machine learning's prevailing constraints. Reinforcement learning powered AlphaGo to conquer the ancient game of Go using solely reward optimization without human exemplars or domain knowledge. One-shot learning algorithms aim to generalize concepts from as few examples as people intrinsically can, while generative adversarial networks surface training blind spots. Combined with increased model transparency, there exist paths for machine learning to transcend its otherwise myopic mastery toward broadly intuitive, self-reflective and transferrable artificial intelligence across changing contexts.

The Ongoing Quest Towards Artificial General Intelligence

Since its origins seven decades ago, machine learning has traversed a non-linear odyssey, navigating multiple pivotal eras—the preliminary neural network architectures of the 1950s through 1960s, stagnation during the first AI winter in the 1970s, redemption through backpropagation and statistical learning in the 1980s and 1990s, and the deep learning revolution of the 2010s. This journey reflects the fits and starts of ambitious scientific exploration through both stagnant periods and accelerated progress catalyzed by insight convergence across mathematics, neuroscience, psychology and engineering.

Each breakthrough and barrier surmounted continues loosely stitching together the patchwork quilt towards the open grand goal of flexible, human-level artificial general intelligence. And while current technologies remain fragile outside narrowly constrained environments, the exponential trajectory signaling future prospects maintains momentum as ever more resources flood into novel machine learning modalities. When observing the angle of progress carved out from stacked layers of vision laid by pioneers onto giants striding ahead today, the ascent toward increasingly capable cognition encoded in substrates of silicon rather than carbon appears inevitable.

Though timescales and ultimate limits to artificial intelligence remain uncertain, the intrinsic human drive to replicate our mysteries in constructed mirrors of ourselves persists unchecked. Machine learning stands poised today at the frontier, ushering in a succession of enhanced capacities via programmed perception, analysis and synthesis, echoing facets of life's own accumulated learning throughout eons of evolution. What these expanding algorithmic intelligences may someday disclose back to us about biomechanisms animating even modest biological cognition, time alone will tell. But the voyage ahead, fueled by humanity's own self-reflected dreams, seems bound to sail deeper into revelations about the computational crux undergirding mortal thoughts and beyond.

Chapter Six

Language, Logic, and AI

The Linguistic and Logical Pillars Supporting Artificial Intelligence

The ascending arc of artificial intelligence draws momentum from twin disciplines focused on processing structures underlying human cognition: the interpretation of natural language and the formal manipulation of symbolic logic. Language and logic enable articulating ideas for communication and reasoning, whether for interpersonal exchange or internal contemplation. By capturing these faculties computationally to analyze tasks and contexts, solve problems, take actions and articulate explanations, systems gain higher-order intelligence governable by transparent rules rather than opaque machine code intricacies.

The contributions tracing from linguistic and logical origins throughout AI's unfolding inform both seminal conceptual milestones and the daily ubiquity of contemporary digital assistants. Tracing this parallel momentum reveals interwoven threads binding progress between the two pillars through mutual illumination.

Language Processing: Teaching Machines to Understand Meaning

Algorithms capable of navigating the ambiguity-ridden landscape of human languages have compounded multiple innovations over the decades toward managing systems with thousands of fluidly interconnected edge cases rather than cleanly delineated inputs and outputs. This journey begins even pre-computationally, with efforts to structure language mathematically.

The 17th-century grammarian Noam Chomsky formulated generative grammar—declarative rule sets capable of explaining the assembly and well-formedness of allowable word combinations in natural sentences. Representing syntax computationally became feasible using Chomsky's formalizations alongside dictionary meanings. Winograd schemas template a methodology for testing understanding by resolving ambiguous pronoun references correctly based on assumed common sense knowledge, posing challenges for computers even today.

When digital computers emerged in the 1950s, these elements allowed basic conversational programs like ELIZA to sustain reasonable exchanges by simply rearranging key terms from user input phrases into new questions to encourage dialog rather than truly understanding exchanges. Yet limitations prompting repetitions exposed the need for deeper meaning.

Core areas maturing include segmentation of speech into words and sentence units via hidden Markov models, tagging parts of speech to decode syntax, parsing sentence structures and even modeling metaphors and emotional affect. Statistical techniques like latent semantic analysis and latent Dirichlet allocation help situate words and documents into contextual themes.

Most impactfully, machine learning breakthroughs since 2010 around recurrent neural networks and powerful transformer architectures have learned linguistic patterns from vast textual data at scales inexpressible through manual rules. Language models like GPT-3 now churn contextual prose given only minimal prompts, while advanced voice recognition and synthesis close perception-reaction loops.

Language in both spoken and written forms remains a grand challenge for AI compared to narrower perceptual domains given infinitely nuanced human expression. Yet steady advances on multiple fronts integrate linguistic knowledge into interactive pathways.

Symbolic Logic: Formalizing the Patterns of Reason

Where language understanding aims to extract meanings, symbolic logic provides fixed semantic meaning to constructs in rule-governed frameworks emulating rigorous reasoning. Instead of vagueness, logical formalisms manage to prove statements unambiguously true or false based on axiomatic primitive facts and explicit deduction protocols.

Digital logic gates undergirding computation itself manifest directly from Boolean algebra's logical operators. More expansive rule systems manipulate chained formal assertions as mathematical proofs proceeding from initial axioms. Expert systems encode complex human analysis into machine inference by mapping industry taxonomies and reasoning shortcuts as symbolic inputs and transformations.

Pioneering efforts include Newell and Simon's Logic Theorist from 1956, which applied axiomatic first principles to systematically derive mathematical proofs through coded procedural knowledge. By representing connections between elements as structured symbols, logical inference is chained through branching paths. This architecture demonstrated learning through self-improvement beyond manual prescription.

Limitations around computational complexity and combinatorial explosion checking exhaustive paths fueled statistically accelerated machine learning as alternatives. But logical formalisms provide transparency absent in numerical methods. Modern techniques integrate neural pattern recognition with structured ontologies and symbolic programming, allowing hybrid neuro-symbolic reasoning. The strengths combine: fluid associations, causal analysis and explanatory capacity. Logical specification channels flexible adaptation, avoiding overfitting quirks common with purely data-driven methods.

Together, linguistic and logical advancements propel artificial intelligence through twin regenerative cycles: language-driven applications deployed at global scale that gather data for improving models and affirming logically formatted knowledge formalized into flexible programs, reaching unprecedented problem-solving sophistication once mathematically intractable. This interplay continues to unfold synthetic intellect.

A Glimpse at the State of AI Assistants Today

The symbiotic maturation of language alongside logic manifests visibly in AI digital assistants like Siri, Alexa and Watson permeating daily experience. These personified interfaces demonstrating key faculties sketched by visionaries over the past decades highlight integrated convergence.

At the front end, automatic speech recognition (ASR) algorithms decode audio input into text for interpretation. Text and meaning get passed on to dialogue managers, who determine appropriate responses based on sensed contextual cues. Vocal synthesizers translate chosen actions back into speech for seamless voice-driven conversations.

Under the hood, recurrent and convolutional deep neural networks parse speech signals and identify triggers. Transformer text bots pull responses from indexed data or generate new phrases. Task delegation APIs connect media controls and query engines. Explicit knowledge graphs overlay situational awareness through networked symbolic concepts. And orchestration layers optimize and track dialogue progress using planning algorithms and policy learning.

Collective tooling mirrors high-level cognition functionally: perceiving environmental stimuli, interpreting informational chunks, filtering meaningless noise, activating memories by contextual association, evaluating conceptual relationships and consequences from known facts, and directing adaptive behaviors toward internal goals. Incremental progress on each capability continues to advance integrated assistance intelligence.

On the Horizon: Domain Versatility and Generalizability

While modern AI achieves or exceeds human performance at narrow disciplinary tasks, from chess playing to particle physics, expanding competence across varied subjects and intuitive adaptation to novel environments remain lacking. The next horizon targets transfers beyond siloed applications toward generalizable reasoning.

Multimodal model architectures seek this flexibility by jointly processing signals across image, text, voice and other modes. Meta-learning algorithms build higher-level learning frameworks to unlock new domain assimilation faster from a few examples, like human infant development. And composability using declarative programming paradigms over monolithic flows better contains component interactions. By using symbolic knowledge with current empirical methods, we can get closer to creating hybrid neuro-symbolic systems that behave in a more reliable and comprehensible way.

Measuring progress quantitatively also presents open problems using metrics like schema variance, cross-domain validation and contextual drift detection that remain roughly defined. Work here increases confidence in capabilities beyond narrowly contrived assessments.

Conclusion: Standing on Linguistic Shoulders Towards Broad AI

From the onset of AI exploration, researchers identified language and logic as central pillars of human cognition and key frontiers for computerization. Early invention blueprint concepts are still propelling current exponential progress in automated speech recognition, neural machine translation and context awareness.

Parallel rule-based and statistical learning traditions managed gradual approximations toward fluid expression and reasoning comparable to people. Pioneering displays of individual skills were balanced by times of group failure, but over time, integrated skills were developed through methodical scientific accumulation.

Each paradigm individually cracked long withstanding barriers around the fluidity of human language or the complexity of orchestrated reasoning. In symbiosis, continuous improvement iterates towards the grand goal of systems exhibiting increasingly versatile, common sense intelligence at scale by integrating the twin methodologies undergirding all intelligent thought: comprehending the present based on remembered concepts and deciding future actions based on their expected outcomes.

Standing on the shoulders of pioneers reaching toward this mountain summit, this groundbreaking work feels the apex within tangible proximity even as the final human parity milestones linger obscured behind passing clouds hovering around the next ridge, waiting to be grasped by outstretched hands pulling the rest behind toward the last base camp, separating imagination from reality. How closely the thought- and language-infused systems manifesting today will stand shoulder-to-shoulder with people tomorrow as peers rather than tools remains unseen. But the view looking upward feels nearer by the day as we traverse steep slopes together.

Chapter Seven

Cold War Era

The Cold War Crucible: Geopolitics and the Forging of Early Artificial Intelligence

T he cauldron of geopolitical tensions boiling between erstwhile allies in the post-WWII era forged unusual ingredients together, baking foundational progress in computational techniques that would ultimately spawn artificial intelligence as we know it. The perceived threat of impending conflict stimulated investment in automated computation for security purposes. This drive toward tactical supremacy demanded pioneering work connecting human and machine cognition to analyze complex situations, culminating in applications both defense-oriented and beyond.

The Race to Match Technological Prowess

The Soviet Union's launch of Sputnik on October 4, 1957, galvanized the United States as the first artificial satellite placed in orbit, marking perceived American weakness in space technology and rocketry. A burgeoning communist rival demonstrating this engineering capacity prompted fears around significant capability asymmetry considered a national vulnerability.

The competitive innovation environment of the subsequent Cold

War, spanning over three decades, was characterized by acute sensitivities toward any gaps allowing opponents to achieve dangerous strategic edges from intelligence to warfare. Both nations invested heavily in scientific initiatives that could yield security applications, with lavish funding attracting top talent toward fields offering outsized resources.

Areas with potential military implications like photography, propulsion, information technology and communication networks received major backing. Artificial intelligence, with its prospects for transforming analysis and decision-making through computational emulation or augmentation of human faculties, joined this high-priority technological front among allied engineering efforts in computing necessary to manifest machine-enabled cognition.

Mobilizing Research and Funding in AI

In response to apparent technical ground ceded following Sputnik alongside general Cold War pressures, the United States government pursued various structural initiatives to accelerate research and consolidate brainpower aimed at national security capabilities. The 1957 launch of Sputnik created the perception that the Soviets had gained an advantage by harnessing scientific progress closer to defense needs. This helped motivate legislation like the 1958 National Aeronautics and Space Act which founded NASA and also DARPA, which was nested under the new Advanced Research Projects Agency (ARPA) within the Department of Defense.

The mandate of agencies like DARPA and ARPA included preventing future technological surprises from endangering national security by better unifying military leadership with research directions across channels like academia. The focus centered on organizing interdisciplinary breakthroughs from fields as diverse as materials science, energy systems and information processing around applications offering force multiplication like command and control or automated sensing and response. AI's versatility, spanning areas from sensor fusion to predictive analysis, made it a natural candidate.

From the 1960s onward, lavish funding allowed rapid prototyping of bullish visions termed "machine intelligence" at research hubs like MIT, Carnegie Mellon and Stanford, along with intimate consulting relationships with military agenda-setters. This capital-flooded effort attracted talent and catalyzed advances in crucial hardware like interactive time-sharing computer interfaces alongside software innovations in programming tools, operating systems and most critically, theories around AI itself. The enriched funding environment helped actualize the digital computation capabilities necessary to transcend purely theoretical speculation around machine-based reasoning into practical experimentation.

Pursuing Military Applications

The significantly accelerated development pace of AI drew inspiration in part from analogous human cognitive processes used by security analysts or strategists but restructured for computerization. Automating tasks like detecting signatures in sensor data, tracing communication between monitored entities, simulating hypothetical scenarios or filling information gaps all promised to bolster decision support and lighten the cognitive burden around complexity, uncertainty and information overload, which innately challenge human operators.

Areas receiving major investment included war gaming environments that conducted battlefield simulations to uncover tactics and countermoves using automated reasoning. Machine learning research toward pattern recognition and classification of radar signatures as friend or foe faced real-time performance constraints. Natural language processing served needs in machine translation and coded communication reduction. IMAGE RECOGNITION IMAGE RECOGNITION Speech and character recognition drove human-computer interaction with autonomous commanders. Expert systems codified rules around munitions deployment and logistics. And novel basic science explored the boundaries of what computation itself could manifest.

Behind the security curtain, rumors abound of more unorthodox or morally dubious applications like automated interrogation systems, predictive mass surveillance algorithms flagging dissenters and autonomous data falsification for propaganda manufacturing lurking on black project ledgers as well. However, the aggregate critical mass forming around government-sponsored AI crucially fueled overall progress widely distributed among commercial, academic and open source channels beyond exclusively governmental usage.

Global Dispersion Beyond Initial Sparring Poles

The Soviet-American rivalry represented the most dramatic faceoff, energizing early AI research for security objectives. But the transformational nature of computational technology, even in its earliest instantiations, could not remain isolated across the Iron Curtain divide for long. Automation and information processing give businesses a productivity edge. This meant that AI would spread around the world, either by espionage or by competitors working together.

Research programs outside Moscow and the Pentagon soon bloomed in European quarters like England's University of Edinburgh alongside Asian centers such as the Indian Institute of Science catalyzed by their own strategic necessity and commercial potential. Japan in particular mobilized AI and robotics efforts in the 1960s from industrial impetus to release human talent from manufacturing drudgery toward more innovative roles.

Despite moments of geopolitical flare-up like the Cuban Missile Crisis, which raised tensions during Nikita Khrushchev's leadership, the overarching Cold War conflict maintained an equilibrium of implicit mutual destruction, encouraging selective transparency around intentions to avoid terminal miscalculation. This permeable antagonism enabled managed cooperation in fields like space exploration, leading to the 1975 Apollo-Soyuz joint mission. Such initiatives allowed occasional exchange, illuminating common challenges using technological bridges even amidst ideological walls. Within limits, pioneering concepts around optimization algorithms or machine learning architectures could be transmitted internationally through avenues like academic conferences rather than battle plans or weapons schematics.

The Pursuit Branching Beyond Conflict

The vigorous incubation climate across American and Soviet laboratories, driven by security ambitions, undoubtedly accelerated progress in computational techniques core to manifesting machine intelligence. Yet due to its underlying versatility, AI research fueled by conflict interests gradually diffused beyond military applications over time.

The thawing of Cold War apprehensions by the late 1980s opened space for commercial development on a large scale. Lessons around data modeling and knowledge representation from classified programs primed adaptations suited for business use cases. The rise of personal computing platforms like the Macintosh 128K, which hosts common productivity software, heralded the migration from room-sized mainframes to desktops.

The 1990s transition into peace and market globalization allowed internet proliferation. Suddenly, massive information sets (hexagrams) requiring learning algorithms to extract signals from noise emerged, ready for mining using neural networks and support vector machines. As distributed computation advanced, so did demands for intuitive interfaces, predictive analytics and automated decisioning, which are now commonplace. AI, whose technical seeds scattered amidst missile-cast shadows ultimately found sunlight by the close of the 20th century, realigning fears of machine hubris as partners rather than rogue entities we now rely upon daily.

The Geopolitical Catalysts Seeding an Indispensable Revolution

Today, artificial intelligence permeates global infrastructure so thoroughly that its impulses operate invisibly through recommendation engines, supply chains, power grids and medical diagnoses, steering modern civilization. This firmly embedded status quo once resembled moonshot fantasy during the Cold War birthing days, when machine intellect remained imagined rather than instantiated through billions of devices. Without the cultivated threats between two superpowers channeling resources into embryonic imaginings, early visions may have dematerialized as abandoned mirages for lack of sustaining nurture.

The mutual escalation dynamics birthed from postwar victory realignments—while hazardous due to annihilation risks—proved fertile for technological progress by explicitly manifesting the fears of an adversary outpacing its abilities. This tangible specular nemesis demanded researchers formalize and instantiate theories into prototypes, exploring the possible lest bold opponents seize advantage on some unexpected nonviolent front through engineering acumen or electronic ingenuity.

This tense study of opposing moves and countermoves crystallized greater mutual understanding, illuminated not by transient facts but by lasting truths undergirding both Eisenhower's military-industrial complex and Khrushchev's scientific aspirations for communism. In particular, the revelation that acquiring and applying knowledge itself for creation and efficiency remains the domain of tool builders rather than fighters sets constructors apart as fundamental agents beyond any particular ideology. Out of distrust and caution against destructive surprises, digital assistants and pandemic resilience were born.

The Cold War condensed ambient tensions between rival ideologies into acute this-or-that scenarios powered by dreams of definite supremacy. But unintended legacies echoing after blast waves settled came to dominate former terms of measurable strength like stockpiles and missiles. Technologies like computational prediction, language translation and even the internet's underlying packet relay structure arose from intellectual mobilization to outsmart, decode and surveil threats and soon turned toward progress and possibility. By channeling work from commercial distraction toward existential necessity, the doomsday polarization paradoxically forged artificial intelligence as a luminous peacekeeper, now continuing to expand cooperation through the learning machines it brought to life after the dust cleared.

Chapter Eight

AI Winters

Navigating the AI Winters: Cycles of Boom and Bust on the Long Road to Progress

The trajectory of artificial intelligence traces an uneven path, navigating peaks and valleys as progress intermittently accelerates and retreats. Periodic "AI Winters" denote the troughs when funding dried up and skepticism mounted around promises seen sliding further over the horizon. Yet the forced reassessment and direction change during these fallow times proved essential for laying sturdy foundations supporting future growth.

The boom and bust cadence reflects inflated expectations around quickly replicating multifaceted markers of biological cognition like flexible reasoning, creativity and common sense within simplified software architectures. However, the complexity of orchestrating interconnected low-level machine operations into higher-order general intelligence repeatedly humbles aggressive timelines. The subsequent disillusionment became an inevitable tax on the compounding upward potential of AI research.

The First Creeping Winter in the Mid-1970s

The earliest strains of AI blossomed with McCarthy's 1956 Dartmouth

Conference and pioneering efforts like Newell and Simon's General Problem Solver rules engine alongside McCarthy's own Lisp programming language. Grand visions of near-human-level machines powered a flowering of investment and startups. However, performances fell short of futurist projections about replicating cerebral functions.

Funding agencies like DARPA in the US and Britain's Science Research Council that had supported 1960s AI labs at Stanford and MIT began pulling back in the 1970s. Venture capital and acquisitions similarly retracted as disquiet grew around meager, usable output. The capabilities demonstrated remained narrow, rigid and devoid of common sense expected of a system claiming intelligence, much less consciousness.

Empirically, while Shakey the Robot could haltingly navigate small spaces and block worlds like SHRDLU could manipulate toy vocabulary universes, the constraints imposed by limited memory, brittle symbolic manipulation and the inability to process natural environments left yawning gaps in human parity. Deep deficiencies in adapting logic to variable real-world contexts became apparent.

This credibility gap between touted expectations and lusterless implementations triggered retrenchment. Budgets and enthusiasm drained as sentiment turned. Labs shuttered and conferences shrank rather than continuing growth trends. An air of unreality pervaded the bulk of AI research directions. The market correction was sharp and sudden, even if seedlings below surface soil continued drawing sustenance.

Regrouping After Disappointment in the Late 1980s

A second winter descended in the late 1980s as success failed to materialize again on projected timelines. The 1970s knowledge systems boom tricked more marginal researchers without rigor into rebranding mundane algorithmic projects as "expert systems," chasing funding bubbles. When these efforts failed to deliver business value after troubled deployments, confidence plunged anew.

Japanese devotion to AI had risen in the Fifth Generation era with projects like specialized Lisp machines and logic programming. But the swollen promises and lack of actual intelligent applications taken for granted today turned investment chill by the 1990s. The expert system bust left researchers masterful in arcane domains like botanical taxonomy yet unable to transfer capabilities later considered routine adaptation.

The low-lying years entering the 1990s thus marked a period of reduced appetite and a sense of unfulfilled potential. Laboratories saw budgets contract, and some corporations, like Atari Research, spun off groups as interest generally waned. The human benchmark continually outpaced programs, with nuanced language, dynamic planning and common sense inferencing firmly out of reach. Deep Blue's calculation of chess combinations was an outlier rather than an indicator of holistic aptitude.

Reemergence Through the Internet's Data Floodgates

Fortuitously, the very next decade heralded redemption as the maturation of computational hardware, the accession of the global internet, and new machine learning algorithmic frameworks converged to unpack AI's previously bottled potential. The influx of data and pervasive connectivity, providing labelled examples at unprecedented scale, powered revitalization.

Distributed systems like Apache Hadoop tamed big data. Advances in neural networks and support vector machines have discovered signals in the noise. Natural language and computer vision results soon reflected refined strategies to narrow human-machine disparity. Venture funding between 2010 and 2015 rebuilt years lost to former winter seasons as startups rode breakthrough applications in speech recognition, autonomous driving, game mastery and digital assistants.

However, some researchers maintain that upswings, ultimately tracing back to the thoughtful realignment and domain focus encouraged during fallow periods, still divide genuine general intelligence, exhibiting adaptable reasoning, from specialized artificially narrow intelligence. But the APP punctuation, which is continually reaching new heights, still blinks a bit further at each crest.

Essential Course Correction: Forcing Introspection

The renewed chill settling periodically on AI development phases proved essential in multiple ways for concentrated progress. Beyond simply consolidating duplicate efforts, the pauses served introspective purposes, realigning trajectories toward realistic deliverables.

The failure aroma stimulated serious inquiry into core assumptions and the distracted conformity common in crowded hype cycles. Pressure-tested ideas exposing limitations under strain highlighted structural gaps in methodologies otherwise papered over by lavish budgets. Back to basic approaches regained appeal, clarifying choices between competing tactics at these junctions.

Returning to theoretical first principles and picking simpler starters over showy long passes rebuilt firmer foundations in areas like probabilistic machine learning and neural network architectures that later bore fruit, accelerating further innovation. The compelled phase changes concentrated direction along fertile lines, which paid compound dividends later. In effect, the wintry respites storing potential energy ultimately boosted future accomplishments.

And the tempered environment encouraged cultural maturation within the field itself as inflated individual profiles and predictions were challenged by hard data. Grandstanding gave way to balanced perspective, with both eyes cognizant of long roads ahead. This healthy skepticism formed immune resistance against future disillusionment. The field emerged more cumulative and integrative from gathering the best ideas forged in cooled settings.

The Cycle Continues Channeling Boom and Bust

The Sisyphean cycle of inflated expectations followed by plunged disillusionment only to climb again seems almost intrinsic to how people and systems grow, whether markets or technology. Periodic excesses inevitably overshoot near-term reality Checks before foundations solidify adequately appreciating the difficulty in securing new territory.

Yet the trajectory through these oscillating modes ultimately trends upward, even as the swings threaten dramatic reactions in both directions. The low points focus attention and reorient attempts toward the most promising pathways. When conditions align favorably again, domains regained lie further up the mountain, even if the summit remains obscured.

AI's uneven progress pathway reflects this punctuated equilibrium. The heady optimism of the 1960s far outpaced actual methodological rigor. The two winters that followed tempered prospects but led research into a more grounded understanding of probabilistic tools. The data computing windfall that commenced around 2010 then unlocked accomplishments that standalone projects could not approach, like computer vision, game mastery and intelligible language processing.

But even as today's AI renaissance powered by deep learning drives toward trillion-dollar predictions, researchers acknowledge the narrowness of the underlying behaviors that are masterful in specific niches yet still clumsy in open worlds requiring adaptable reasoning and common sense. Perhaps another winter is already gathering shadows as expectations chase exponential hardware gains while theories stall around generalizing innate context beyond presently ossified networks.

The boom bust continuum persists as a driving dialectic into unknown territory - irrational exuberance ultimately met with sober prudence and disciplined execution before transcendent imagination takes flight once more. Through this cycle, artificial intelligence gradually actualizes audacious dreams into firm capability building upon setbacks as the essential balancing pole keeping eyes on the distant prize.

Chapter Nine

Rise of Extended Reality

Virtual Reality

The Winding Road to Virtual Reality: From Speculative Fiction to Immersive Technology

T he impulse to construct simulated worlds permeates human creativity, crossing the expanse separating imagination from engineering. Virtual reality exemplifies this migration, which has transpired over centuries from fanciful conjecture into digital fabrication. Today's head-mounted panoramas immerse surprised senses, yet the concept itself enjoys lineage stretching through philosophy thought experiments, theatrical deception, experimental cinema, speculative literature and proto-digital hacking.

That kernel—to synthesize sensoria suspending patrons in substitute spaces—retained allure across eras even as supporting arts gradually manifested required facets. The technological violin capturing attention today is slowly assembled from disparate mediated visions gathered through interwoven moments of inspiration traversing the uncertain terrain linking creativity with science.

Early Conceptual Seeds in Philosophy and Illusionism

Speculation around manufactured reality predates computation itself, indicating innate intrigue with transcending mortal senses toward more malleable planes of being. The notion of fallible perceptions failing to fully apprehend the complete essence of existence appeared alongside enduring inquiries into the underlying nature of reality. if even wakeful experiences could prove deceptive, how to trust the veracity of one's interpreted surroundings? Perhaps a greater architect or evil demon created the consistent illusion of the world?

In his seminal 1641 Meditations on First Philosophy, mathematician and philosopher René Descartes entertained the notion that some malicious entity was systematically misleading his understanding of reality through persistent deception designed to permanently confuse mind and actuality. This framing of radical doubt imagined an artificial reality dynamically fabricated to trick a protagonist - an early version of the simulation hypothesis pondering perceived reality as subterfuge.

The concept of crafting sensorially misleading artifice also traces through stage magic engineering elaborate contraptions confounding observation. Innovators like Jean Eugène Robert-Houdin and John Nevil Maskelyne pioneered moving picture apparatuses and levitation effects that dazzled and deceived theatergoers. These mass illusions portended manufactured perceptions, soon simulating whole realities rather than just isolated trick moments.

Early Cinematic Visionaries Experiment with Immersion

As photographic and moving picture techniques advanced in precision replicating scenes through celluloid in the early 20th century, some pioneers recognized new experiential possibilities in surrounding audiences with images deliberately evoking responses beyond passive viewership. Rather than containing visual data within boxy frames, images could flood fields of vision, foreshadowing today's expansive digital vistas.

In the late 1930s, New York World's Fair exhibitor Somoza Leveridge designed the Telesphere Mask panoramic console, enclosing sightlines with early 360-degree commercial films. Subsequent systems like the Cinerama widescreen theater, featured wrap-around curved projection screens, further boosting immersion. This fusion of realistic cinematography with encompassing presentation sought to maximize the feeling of presence within far-off filmed events, yet it lacked the surrounding depth perception or interactivity possible with later electronics.

However, the most direct forerunner for contemporary virtual reality remained the Sensorama device, invented in the late 1950s. Renowned cinematographer Morton Heilig envisioned an automated theater experience combining stereo speakers, aromatomizers, seat tilters and 3D visuals in a cabinet viewed through binocular optics. His insight united multi-sensory input with first-person perspective within a self-directed device, long anticipating the portable all-in-one headsets that define the modern VR form factor. Sensorama impressed audiences, but its analog approach forestalled replication at consumer product scale. The fruits of its inventive DNA would synthesize properly decades later through digital means.

Literary and Scientific Imaginations Shape Possibilities

Speculative thought experiments around manufactured worlds populate science fiction literature, pushing readers to expand their considerations of reality's essence. Thought leaders called upon escapist fantasy to smuggle philosophy into popular discourse, coloring notions of where existence's solidity ends and mutable artifices begin. Though fantastical, breeding such memes penetrated anticipation for the late-blooming hybridization with electronics.

In his 1935 short story Pygmalion's Spectacles, Stanley Weinbaum conjured a fictional Holcon apparatus using radio waves to transport users into holographic worlds with sight, sound and touch fully simulated. Ray Bradbury's 1950 The Veldt conceived nursery walls projecting interactive, lifelike African plains responsive to thought. Philip K. Dick, Arthur C. Clarke, and dozens of other authors infused tropes around alternate planes that enchanted wider imaginations.

Scientific prophets peered beyond fictional abstraction toward technical possibility, lending pragmatic credence to virtual worlds ascending from fantasy into eventual prototypes. Mathematician John von Neumann's 1951 Lectures on Advanced Computer Science discussed self-reproducing automata perceivable as reality. He detailed hypothetical universal constructor models, making immersive simulation plausible through relentless technological growth. Experiments around networked supercomputers, head tracking and stereoscopic telepresence through the 1960s at the University of Utah seeded less speculative apparatuses.

Early Headset and Glove Exemplars Materialize

The envelope-pushing cycles between speculative science fiction possibilities and emerging electronic possibilities ultimately bore working pilot exemplars of elementary virtual reality capabilities by the mid-1980s. These initial creations outlined templates for refining successor designs, benefiting from accelerating computational power, accessible to wider commercial deployment in coming decades.

At VPL Research, inventor Jaron Lanier coined the enduring term "Virtual Reality" while pioneering early headsets, sensor gloves and programming techniques for interactive motions. Converting speculative questions into demonstrations proved foundational for opening new research avenues and stoking popular interest needed to propel additional development. The creations were still crude yet undeniably alien artifacts, beckoning a broader understanding of reality's malleable boundary.

Research institutions like NASA then forged ahead, improving head tracking speed, display resolution and wired glove responsiveness for applications like telerobotic control. However, costs exceeding hundreds of thousands of dollars restricted systems to elite industrial usage rather than the consumer realm, despite growing cultural curiosity through science fiction depictions in films like The Lawnmower Man. It took the distributed computing revolution before necessary video processing and motion capture powers permeated affordable platforms.

The Digital Cambrian Explosion into Virtual Worlds

Once exponential gains in semiconductor densities began reliably doubling transistor counts, allowing desktop processors to cross power thresholds required for fluid virtual environment rendering, VR finally transcended isolated workstations, migrating toward ubiquitous devices sold at consumer scale. The groundwork fusion between digital sight and sound and human movement, continuously forged by pioneers over a half century, suddenly paid compounding dividends.

When id Software's 1992 Wolfenstein 3D first demonstrated swift texture-mapped first-person exploration powered by consumer graphics cards, VR demonstrations gained renewed momentum. By 2016, the race had culminated between the Oculus Rift and HTC Vive headsets, which delivered compact, high-resolution motion-tracked stereoscopic displays with accompanying hand controllers permitting touch gestures in fully immersive spaces calculated in real-time. Augmented by noise-canceling headphones and wireless flexibility, the result stands miles from crude 1950s motion simulators, yet their DNA lives on, greatly enhanced.

The Future: Towards Ubiquity Through Next-Generation Digital Worlds

While modern virtual reality still appears rooted in novelty stages relative to its total imaginative promise bespoke by visionaries, momentum clearly trended from speculative origins toward an increasingly tangible staple capability improving in cost, accessibility and realism logarithmically faster than any previous visual medium transformation before it. Photography took half a century to reach global ubiquity. Cinema required decades more before extended color and sound blockbusters became routine entertainment. However, video games raced from research curiosities like Spacewar! to global sensation phenomenon with Pong and Mario in barely twenty years as electronics allowed exponential capability leaps.

Immersive digital reality following this trajectory thus seems poised to infiltrate daily life even faster than preceding visual inventions transformed societies thanks to its synthetic nature unconstrained by physical filming limitations. Indeed, many global citizens already access primitive virtual worlds routinely through video conferencing apps, augmented reality filters and mass multiplayer online games forecasting the inevitability of full smooth motion captured simulations entering the mainstream once infrastructure catches up with aspirations.

When networked populations can meet indistinguishably from immediate proximity and collaboratively alter persistent environments, vestiges tethering virtuality to the physical may dissolve, leading to new phase spaces governed by imagination rather than geography. Perhaps future generations will view reality not through literal lenses but through chosen vistas that bridge dreams into reality. In many ways, the ultimate vision behind virtual reality still lays over horizons obscured from the present plateau, yet faith in its eventual arrival persists and is maintained through past seers, nourishing perpetual yearning until science delivers substance.

Chapter Ten

Morton Heilig

Sensorama

Sensorama: The Multi-Sensory Precursor to Virtual Reality

O ver half a century before compact headsets transported gog-gle-wearing patrons into immersive virtual dimensions, an ob-scure arcade cabinet gave visitors a glimpse into digitally simulated worlds using a menagerie of fans, screens and aroma dispensers to substitute senses. This creation, called the Sensorama, conveyed il-lusory experiences more vividly than any medium previously by stim-ulating multiple faculties simultaneously.

Though never reaching commercial success itself, the pioneering device envisioned critical concepts that define virtual reality domains now maturing into ubiquity three decades later. Sensorama and its eccentric inventor, Morton Heilig, illuminated transformational pos-sibilities on the cusp between cinema and computation that resonate through immersive technologies today.

Sensorama's Design: An Analog Assault on the Senses

Morton Heilig graduated from the Art Center College of Design in 1947 and quickly established renown as a Hollywood cinematographer, heading technical film innovation for 20th Century Fox during the industry's lush Technicolor era. His appetite for expanding viewer immersion led him to abandon safe studio confines to chase ideas that were less constrained.

His first invention, Teleview, leveraged motorized optics, mechanically enhancing the cinemascope's immediacy. But seeing limitations in solely visual approaches, Heilig's ambitions escalated toward engineering a full sensory experience machine he labeled Sensorama, seeking to graduate passive viewership into active multi-dimensional participation by recruiting additional senses.

The Sensorama device took shape as a large futuristic cabinet with a binocular viewfinder, handlebars, a vibrating chair, wind fans and tubes dispensing aromas. Users sat within the contraption, gripped controls and watched special films with separate feeds routing to the eyes, ears, nose and skin. The elaborate construction aimed to trick participants into believing they teleported virtually into depicted scenes thanks to combined vision, stereo sound, scents, breezes and seat rumbles.

Though unconventional, Sensorama sold the illusion of riding a real motorcycle in Brooklyn far more convincingly than 2D silent footage and gave viewers an embodied sense of presence in another place by coordinating sensory data into a synchronous artificial world, predating notions of fully immersive virtual reality by decades. Heilig also understood that reptilian faculties like smells uniquely cue recollection, anchoring mental associations through this linkage.

Yet despite the pioneering concept, Sensorama's mechanical nature hampered reliability at the scale needed for commercial venues. Only a single user could experience the coordinated simulation at once. Still, glimpse demonstrations proved profoundly influential over time by demonstrating technological potential to upgrade world representation beyond what nature directly provides our native senses.

Impact on the Development of Virtual Reality

Though initial reactions marked Sensorama as a novelty rather than a breakthrough, concepts explored fundamentally impacted subsequent strides toward virtually generated worlds once computing power and display techniques progressed. Many strengths and limitations of Heilig's prototype frame challenge further innovation in converting rough drafts into mass market fruition.

On the technical front, coordinating coherent sensory streams remains a non-trivial engineering challenge. Modern headsets tackle this by combining wireless hand motion detection with accelerometers tracking spins and external cameras tracing room motions accurately without lag-inducing nausea. High-resolution stereo displays sweep scenes responsive to movement while surround audio shifts localized sound sources with user orientation.

These capabilities are orders of magnitude more performant and compact than Sensorama's mechanical parts, yet they inherit its insight on reconciling multiple inputs to craft continuous illusory spaces. Companies like Facebook Research still pursue adding more perceptual channels like simulated airflows, humidity and temperature, exploring territory trailblazed by Heilig's initiative.

Sensorama also pioneered tailoring theatrical content explicitly for immersion rather than repurposing traditional cinema as mere visual wallpaper. Modern VR creatives optimize digital environments meant for free-roaming inhabitants rather than passive viewers stuck in seats as the entire staging moves from framed sets toward unlocking staged spaces. As headsets gain adoption beyond early adopters, such bespoke world development remains crucial.

Perhaps Sensorama's most prescient legacy centers on cultivating a provocative-mediated experience that departs from replicating ordinary reality. Heilig understood immersion as transcendent promise rather than just a utilitarian interface improvement. In doing so, he opened imaginations to virtual reality's latent capacity, manifesting fantastical spaces digitally where we transcend physical limits. This aspiration toward the sublime intact fuels Silicon Valley billion-dollar wagers, seeding the current VR renaissance.

Pioneer in His Own Words: Core Tenets Underlying the Tech

Directly extended quotes attributable to Morton Heilig seem scarce given his niche position as an innovator rather than a mainstream celebrity inventor. However, his de facto principles resonate uncannily with digital virtual worlds built decades hence. Though constrained by 1950s technology, Heilig verbalized elements that define an enduring VR ethos:

Experience Theater: Drive to Recruit All Senses Seamlessly

Heilig framed his mission as not seeking bigger visual frames but instead coordinating complete sensory orchestration, saying, "The ultimate motion picture theater will exclude the audience. You will be IN the picture. All your senses will be simultaneously awakened." This insistence that virtuality demands fully integrated environments, not just visual tricks, underpins the immersive agenda.

Subjective Personal Experience: Beyond Wall Watching

He likewise noted that "the formally passive audience assumes active participation," reflecting a focus beyond observational media formats to modes where patrons personally steer experiences filtered subjectively through their own involvement. The centrality of escapist fantasy over passive documentary captures modern gaming and social VR.

Overall, Heilig's principles foreshadowed present aspirations around immersing ourselves in reality layers merging digital fabrication, custom vantage points and augmented sensory data streams. Though sequestered using static apparatus, his vision remains dynamically extensible thanks to exponential hardware gains gradually converting his mechanical proof points into default digital capacities.

Lasting Impact: Inspiring Future Generations of Immersive Tech Innovators

The tricks and gadgets powering Sensorama itself aged rapidly against remorseless computerization trends that outdated legacy kinematics with physics-defying bits manipulable through screens alone. Its before-its-time concept, contradicted by its modest footprint among novelty fans, ultimately could not summon the significant commercial support during the 1960s needed to evolve the prototypes into platforms ready for living rooms.

Yet despite financial setbacks closing Heilig's theater business and driving him from the industry, the numinous visions kindled in audiences exposed to Sensorama's fleeting miracles helped seed a mental runway for digital successors decades ahead that recreated his immersive ambitions on exponentially more capable substrates. When asked what lasting impact his work left generations later, Heilig reflected, "I'm told that I invented Virtual Reality. I didn't invent it so much as try it out, test it, and find out how convincing it was." This acknowledgement as trailblazing experimenter resonates accurately.

Today's embodiment of versatile head-mounted displays paired with wireless handheld controllers and room-mapping cameras culminates in capabilities that Sensorama could only crudely approximate using film prints synchronized across motor-actuated platforms. Yet where Heilig led, showing sensory fusion feasibility beyond theory, now profitable billion-dollar corporations like Meta rushed to capture the immense frontiers opened by his hard-earned insights, finally maturing through pervasive computing.

His signature immersion cabinet now resides behind museum glass as an enshrined prototype rather than an operating artifact due to device obsolescence. But the creative spark behind its inception helped awaken a latent desire for stepping virtually through the screen frame into worlds limited only by imagination—destinations fast materializing today, thanks in part to Heilig first illustrating avenues ahead. In this sense, Sensorama's triumph remains less a technical accomplishment than a conceptual contribution, seeding aspirations and carrying users increasingly deeper down the butterflied reality tunnel it symbolically first breached.

Morton Heilig's pioneering Sensorama work expanded the notion of immersive experience beyond conventional visual mediums by conceptually fusing discrete technological stages into a multi-sensory prototype. The limitations of its era made digitally generated virtual worlds impossible to sustain cost-effectively over networks. However, core insights framing VR as the pursuit of wrapped realities coordinated over enveloping inputs creatively inspire current artists and engineers decoding digital infinity one sense at a time. Past forgotten, future gained.

Chapter Eleven

Ivan Sutherland

Sword of Damocles

The Evolution of Immersive Headsets: Birthing Virtual and Augmented Reality

The trajectory bringing virtual and augmented reality from speculative fancy into demonstrative prototypes owes significantly to early headwear contraptions that first enclosed computer-generated imagery inches from senses. The creative urge manifested through this watershed hardware marks a pivotal leap bridging raw signal into surround sensation that birthed new technological lineages.

Ivan Sutherland and the Sword of Damocles

Before light and form filled goggled sight to transport viewers into alternate spaces, only bold technical visionaries like Ivan Sutherland glimpsed the latent potential underlying networked screens, sensors and minicomputers. In 1965, Sutherland outlined an aspirational Ultimate Display concept in which the computer controls all of reality's visible atoms, conjuring anything imaginable. This vague mixing of environmental elements pointed toward cybernetic worlds but lacked concrete instantiation.

Three years later, while teaching at Harvard, Sutherland collaborated with student Bob Sproull to craft the first working virtual reality head-mounted display (HMD) system, aiming to manifest this goal in microcosm. They constructed an HMD containing twin CRT monitors mounted on a mechanical arm suspended from the ceiling, giving users a stereoscopic 3D view of basic wireframe room environments with the ability to look around by turning their heads.

The bulky device called Sword of Damocles piped vector outlines over predecessors like Heilig's cinema cabinets to become the earliest functional model for surrounding eyes with integrated perspective visuals linked to head motion. It physically embodied the concept of a virtual space that could be navigated freely. The sword moniker poetically evoked the precarious risk latent in escaping reality for cyberspace.

Through multiple technical limitations, Sword of Damocles crucially broke initial ground, demonstrating key principles required for viably immersing patrons in responsive vistas detached from the immediate physical. Yet immense practical problems around unwieldy form factor, controller ergonomics, display resolution, motion tracking precision and modeling complexity persisted for decades before solutions gradually materialized through long interdisciplinary effort.

Augmented Reality Lets Digital Layers Enhance Real Existence

If virtual environments substitute senses entirely with synthetic input, augmented reality alternatively overlays digitally generated data atop still dominant physical stimuli. Visionary pioneers likewise prototyped working HMD systems fusing contextual computer graphics with natural scenes as collaborators sought applications for enhanced environments.

In the early 1990s, Louis Rosenberg developed monocular overlay units for US Air Force testing aids that could project targeting symbols on aircraft windshields to assist fighter pilot performance. This established utility revolves around rendered graphics boosting human operation in complex tasks, bridging data visualization onto real environments. However, bulky battery packs impeded adoption.

Around the year 2000, university researchers made augmented reality more usable and accurate by using touring machine projectors to show on-demand environmental context from backpacks and handheld screens to add annotations to natural views. Advancements continued in the 2010s as smartphones grew powerful enough to capture room images, sense position and overlay timely locative data in real time using just pocket devices.

Applications like visual search, photography enhancement, gaming and navigation demonstrate augmented practicality at the global handset scale. And near-eye improvements, including optical transparency, maintain momentum thanks to interest from giants like Microsoft HoloLens projecting holographic interfaces ahead. Sutherland's grand 1965 conjecture of controllable matter is incrementally more tangible through digital fusion.

Perspectives from Early Pioneers Charting Twin Frontiers

The respective pioneering efforts behind birthing and bootstrapping virtual and augmented headwear modalities into explorable technological directions concentrated mass inspiration, funding and interdisciplinary contributions needed to transform concepts into marketable offerings. Beyond engineering feats, these visionaries verbalized guiding tenets echoed by current industry giants corporatizing their ideas commercially.

Ivan Sutherland's quotes highlight aspirations around digitally unshackled representations blending physical ease with arbitrarily mutable dynamics, saying, "The ultimate display would, of course, be a room within which the computer can control the existence of matter." And on enhanced comprehension beyond mortal vectors: "It is a looking glass into a mathematical wonderland." Together, the creative urge to exceed natural capability and leverage this power for previously impossible modes of understanding rings clear through Sutherland's visions.

The legacy continues to permeate the broader cultural mindset through science fiction visions like the Star Trek Holodeck and films like the Metaverse-themed Ready Player One that borrow heavily from seeds planted by pioneering HMD research. These tropes install yearnings around cybernetic realities manifesting imagined possibility across mass consciousness, building reservoirs of talent and capital accelerating efforts to catch capabilities up with imagination as visionaries peer conceptually far down realistic roads ahead.

Trailblazing Headset Systems Herald the Future of Immersive Reality

Early virtual environment contraptions foreshadowed critical challenges around intuitive ergonomics, wireless freedom, responsive graphics and processing bottlenecks that extensive consumer-level engineering efforts gradually surmounted. Today, multi-billion-dollar companies like Meta and HTC have effectively conquered groundbreaking prototypes developed decades earlier using far more capable modern substrates.

And smartphone-mediated augmented worlds, once viewed as novel gimmicks, now rank as indispensable nationwide infrastructure thanks to GPS navigation and informational augmentations, digitally enhancing everything from routine shopping trips to unprecedented platforms like packed stadium concerts. Sutherland's mathematical wonderland simile proves annually more substantive through this stripe of diversity.

The largest gap persists not in technological capacity but in creativity, definitively exploring seldom-tread possibilities opened once cybernetic-looking glasses progressed from novelty toward normalcy. What new cultural customs, market dynamics and existential risks gather around the horizon as augmented and virtual windows begin outnumbering these typed words as our default vista to the world? Immersive pioneers set the heading—our collaborative navigation lies ahead.

Chapter Twelve

The Evolution of AR

Augmented Reality: The Winding Journey from Concept to Mass Adoption

The notion of digitally overlaying graphical data atop views of physical spaces involved gradual interdisciplinary progress, navigating early imagination toward deployed engineering. Today's heads-up maps and visual product configurators materialize interaction visions pioneering researchers articulated decades prior. Augmented reality transcended conceptual origins as hypothetical user interfaces until mobile devices enabled widespread access by leveraging improved software techniques and hardware capabilities.

Initial Explorations Bridging Physical and Virtual

Speculation of seamless fusing between rendered imagery and environmental sight reaches back to postwar information theorists like Douglas Engelbart musing on augmenting thought itself through interactive screens. Engineers then began earnest experiments toward this goal as early computers enabled primitive graphical injection over external optics.

At the University of Utah circa 1970, professor Dave Evans operated the overlay mapping project, where technicians prototyped early outlining system concepts by filming campus scenery and then manually tracing building floor plans with positional graphics onto the analog footage in real time. This evolving process of mixing physical space with digital annotation portended machine vision-based automated approaches that developed later.

Ivan Sutherland, inventor of the pioneering Sword of Damocles VR headset, also published influential texts outlining his concept for the Ultimate Display, wherein visual digital rendering achieves visual indistinguishability from objects in the real world. This proposal resonates as well with aspirations around amplifying environments by introducing virtual elements intermixed plausibly with unmodified surroundings. However, actual technology remained constrained to traditional, opaque monitors.

Birth of the Term "Augmented Reality" Itself

Serious momentum began crystallizing around situating graphical overlays in live contexts, with Boeing researcher Tom Caudell coining the "augmented reality" term itself in 1990. Caudell came up with the language to describe the difference between external reality supplementation and purely virtualized alternatives while he was the lead researcher on a project to use virtual aid overlays to guide the assembly of airplanes.

Teams then implemented augmented reality assistance concepts into prototype head-mounted display systems for factory workers building wiring bundles. This matched ideal configurations over ongoing construction and increased productivity, like prefigured engineering schematics brought to life through the production floor. Improved comprehension and accuracy resulted from this handy exoskeletal visualization layered contextually over tasks, magnifying human precision and recall via prompts.

The aviation field continued to spearhead adoption of augmented reality situational aids throughout the 1990s, with applications assisting flight lines and diagnostics leveraging see-through displays and positioned notations. Momentum gathered around expanding accessible interfaces between physical effort and digitally enhanced output. But hardware constraints slowed ubiquitous spread until fundamental breakthroughs in mobile processing and cameras unleashed new potential.

The Smartphone Catalyst Unleashing Widespread Augmented Reality

Before scaled augmented reality replaced bespoke implementations on a small scale, the vision needed major software and hardware improvements that happened over decades until smartphones made the phenomenon visible. In particular, several conceptual pillars requiring milestone progress framed what mobile technology mastered through commoditized global devices.

- Algorithms: Efficient computer vision techniques like local feature detection (SIFT, SURF) emerged, recognizing environmental items for registration and modeling real objects in context, critical for credible augmented overlays. Concurrently, graphics chips improved considerably in projecting rendered frames quickly enough over roomy backgrounds at acceptable visual fidelity without lag.

- Displays: Screen technologies upgrading from blocky vintage VR goggles toward lightweight transparent glasses (Vuzix) with cameras permitted blending digital enhancement without blocking ordinary vision. These granted users mobility without encumbrance or isolation from receiving environmental cues.

- Tracking: Sensors like compasses, GPS units and accelerometers provide key signals to calculate posture, orientation and location in the spatial context necessary for plausibly situating overlaid information tied to real objects viewed from various positions over time. Precision equating augmented elements with reality as appearances shift becomes crucial to believable immersion.

- Connectivity: Advances in wireless broadband (3G, LTE) enabled transmitting rich media augmentations in real-time from
  servers rather than confining deployment to what standalone
  hardware configurations could store locally. This massively
  expanded possibilities in dynamic, customized augmentation
  flavors.

The ensemble integration of these progress pillars finally triggered explosive interest in location-based augmented reality, evident
through phenomena like Pokémon GO, which delivered interactive
creatures rendered over neighborhoods across millions of consumer
iPhone devices. This hinted at coming waves of commercial creativity
vindicating decades of assembled infrastructure.

Industrial Roots Now Branch Into Myriad Fields

Boeing's early efforts to use augmented reality to boost worker productivity by adding extra features to headsets were both very useful for
mechanical tasks and a sign of things to come for information overlay
tools in general. Much of the DNA found in those early manufacturing
amplification objectives persists, guiding development today. Remote
assist apps like Microsoft Dynamics 365 allow technicians to collabo-
rate with distant experts using augmentation.

However, radical mobile phone enablement opened exponential
channels beyond limited factory settings toward massively diversified
applications and exploring fresh ideas around digitally modulated environments. Some directly applicable domains include construction
sites overlaying planned staging and architecture. Interior design apps
like IKEA Place populate rooms with lifesize furniture configurations,
testing layout options digitally. Healthcare training clarifies anatomy
and best practices using simulated assets over patients or dummy
targets, highlighting precision.

Speculative realms also gather momentum around augmented
meetings through conferencing ecosystems like spatially anchoring
remote collaborators in virtual spaces with a unified presence. Spa-

tial computing paints a future where persistent digital twinning becomes commonplace, mapped onto our presence. And experimental brain-computer interfaces literally float control panels through imagination alone. Potential remains undiscovered.

Legacy of Early Visionaries and Future Trajectory

Today, Apple ARKit and Google ARCore toolchains are built atop early augmented trailblazing to make environmental annotation easily accessible to coders and creators. The maturing development platforms baseline intuitions researchers spent years bootstrapping to demonstrate enhancing aspects physically possible. And each projection firms more substance behind originating notions verbalized memorably justifying exploratory efforts.

Ivan Sutherland highlighted the unique comprehensibility possible, saying augmentation permitted "looking glass into a mathematical wonderland," where abstract views manifest physically. Early pioneer Myron Krueger believed reality itself could transform into a "malleable medium of expression." through synthetic integration. Tomorrow's creators, empowered to edit and enhance rooms, now bring this flexible agency toward digitally mutable worlds.

The voyage ahead traces from the earliest imagination around flanking our senses with insightful data streams into increasing high-fidelity generation indistinguishable from source reality. Every model honing reference frame coordinates, reducing rendering latency and miniaturizing projection hardware brings that ultimate display where real and imagined converge centrally into view bit by bit.

Chapter Thirteen

Convergence of AI and XR

AI Meets VR and AR

The Convergence of Artificial Intelligence and Immersive Technologies

The trajectory of virtual and augmented reality arcing from speculative fancy into adopted infrastructure owes significantly to artificial intelligence technologies permeating recent systems. AI research itself also relies increasingly on emerging immersive modalities like virtual testbeds, stimulating progress in developing situated agent intelligence. The combination enables unprecedented interactivity, customization and accessibility, transcending limitations previous generations faced.

Rendering Responsive Environments

Virtual environments detach senses from physical law toward realms where imagination supersedes corporeal constraints. Augmented overlays recontextualize scenes by introducing informative elements upon ordinary observation. In the early phases, crude systems operated passively, using canned animations oblivious to user actions except intermittent commands. Their experience felt prescribed along narrow branches rather than alive through dynamic involvement.

Integrating artificial intelligence algorithms that continuously monitor internal states based on environmental data and participant behaviors enables shifting immersion onto more adaptive foundations. If VR worlds model learning capacity responding to visitor choices, limitless possibility unfolds rather than thinly branched narratives. NPC dialogue can reference past discussions, demonstrating recall, while computer vision tracks body language, nudging responses.

Likewise, augmented spaces aware of user identity, gaze and task context via machine perception can situate information adaptively where most relevant without overwhelming limited attention. Object recognition focuses label annotations on items of interest while ignoring distracting backgrounds. Gaze pointers generate composite views, fusing workstation CAD designs with finished assemblies on factory floors and simplifying manufacturing chains. Interpreting user motions and environmental factors supports fluid interplay that is impossible via static overlays.

Synthesizing Situated Voice Interfaces

Language interfacing allows direct articulation of thought for cooperation, replacing fragmented menu navigation or hand gestures that decode intent through multiple steps. Smooth voice exchange creates a seamless feel by concentrating user focus on tasks rather than physical control mechanisms. Augmented telepresence meetings benefit from effortless vocal backchannel chatter. New VR gamers ask aloud for guidance rather than toggling settings, interrupting gameplay.

Underneath, natural language processing handles parsing varied spoken phrases into identified commands, queries and references. Generative subsystems produce responses personalized using identity and conversation history modeling. Emotional tone analysis informs appropriate speech cadence and word choice for friendly machine interaction. Additionally, audio wave propagation modeled spatially across virtual rooms creates realistic immersion through naturally directional voice transmission effects keyed to source proximity and layout materials.

Together, these AI innovations enable situational voice exchange to flow effortlessly as an auxiliary interface scaffolding user objectives rather than signaling technology itself. Reliable speech serves as one of the most intuitive modalities for cooperation between minds when reliably interpreted and answered contextually. Its reciprocity through artificial means expands journeying through imaginary environments jointly rather than alone.

Fostering Realistic Presence Detection

Augmented spaces seeking believable integration with physical environments rely intimately upon AI technologies performing real-time scene understanding to realistically merge real and virtual. The sophistication of computer vision routines for analyzing camera input to identify environmental context correlates directly with augmentation plausibility when anchoring annotations.

Algorithms categorize objects like furniture suites against database labels for annotation automatically, without manual tracking. They similarly recognize building facades and room layouts to estimate precise observer coordinates in scaled space. More exotic techniques decode ephemeral qualities like material textures and ambient lighting to recreate consistent visual properties applied to virtual furniture renderings and animated characters.

Additionally, facial tracking combined with neural network classifiers gauge implicit cues like micro-expressions, revealing user mindset and attitude, used to tune interactions appropriately. Algorithmic perception spanning these facets aims to approach ubiquitous environmental literacy by supporting augmentation algorithms—knowing precisely what, who and where defines the scene before appropriately orienting embedded information. The AI sight harnessing observations to direct responses pushes augmented reality farther toward credible realism.

Procedural Generation and Performance Optimization

Crafting expansive cinematic VR encounters challenges budgets when asset production and environment modeling costs scale exponentially across long-form experiences. Unique gameplay demands in gaming contexts also strain designers, balancing endless novelty against development practicalities. AI-generative algorithms help address both cases by leveraging learning models trained on domain data sets to manufacture original artifacts dynamically customized per user.

Procedural text, geometry, textures and dialogue production schemas are controlled through high-level parameters, which supply creators leverage to control scope while increasing output diversity. Domains given to computational creators include everything from virtual smart city architecture to accessories, clothing, avatar wardrobes and equipping spaceship fleet weaponry.

On the optimization side, AI helps tune graphic fidelity in real time against available rendering processing headroom to maximize visual quality without dropping immersive frame rates. Content-aware adjustment of scene components strikes compromise, balancing key regions or game characters at the highest resolution while simplifying peripheral areas dynamically where quality drops fall subtly.

Together, these adaptive optimization and generative AI routines augment designers facing exponentially expanding creative scope as audiences desire increasing spectacle. Automating hands assists imagination when outpacing individual capacity.

Exploring Shared Social Immersion

Early virtual reality focused on isolating individuals inside non-reactive worlds delivered through goggles, severing outside stimulus. Augmentation conversely anchored users still rooted physically while enhancing rooms with informative splashes unchanged by others present. Artificial intelligence research now targets transcending both models into persistent cyber-physical ecosystems binding people across distances through graphical embodiment and speech interface.

Online multi-user environments like Facebook Horizon construct interpersonal hubs by joining spatially proximate avatars using body tracking, facial capture and real-time voice exchange. Second Life pioneered virtual economies and social hangouts years earlier, but current hardware conveys nonverbal signals, establishing trust through instinctual human rhythms inaccessible previously. And cryptocurrency integration may incentivize compelling worlds by connecting participation with financial opportunity.

These experiments progress toward shared cybernetic spaces, combining the strengths of physical presence with the liberties of programmed environments, possibly exceeding the best of both. The AI required moving forward demands increasingly multifaceted social awareness, speech competence and user modeling, shining past current conversational limitations into the realm of true rapport. Achieving this algorithmically poses a grand challenge.

Pushing Immersion to Its Limits and Beyond

Today's artificial intelligence infusion continues maturing VR and AR technologies along pathways pioneered through initial voice interfaces, reactive experiences and expanded possibilities. Increasingly capable algorithms broaden applications spanning entertainment, design, medicine and beyond—fields once confined to traditional flat screens now unfold into worlds figuratively and literally.

But even near-term AI innovation seems less bounded by conceptual barriers than implementing exponentially growing computational resources, bridging abstractions into economical embodiments at at global scale. So from a practitioner lens, the pragmatic path ahead appears to be charted largely through engineering terrain after architecting the guiding landmarks demonstrating key possibilities. Establishing unified ecosystems will depend more on incremental corporate puzzle assembly regarding UX polish, developer tools and cross-device synchronization than pure research.

Of course, unforeseen ideas ever simmer at the frontiers of undiscovered science, but existing signposts trace toward conversational human parity and photorealistic immersion mirroring life itself through artificial means. The revelations then promised about artificial sentience, creative identity and communal dynamics reshaping post-physical existence offer profound opportunity once technological locks relent through time, investment and collective intent. That unfolding futurity grounds the present pioneering.

Chapter Fourteen

Enhancing Reality

AI in XR

Infusing Immersive Extended Reality Environments with Artificial Intelligence

The trajectory of realizing virtual reality from speculative origins toward adopted infrastructure relies intensely on artificial intelligence technologies permeating recent systems. Increasingly capable algorithms broaden applications spanning entertainment, design, medicine and beyond—domains once confined to traditional flat screens now unfold into worlds figuratively and literally more lifelike thanks to machine learning, computer vision and natural language processing.

AR spaces overlaying graphical information rely on AI to interpret real-time environmental context from images, LiDAR scans, and motion sensors before blending annotations seamlessly. VR environments simulate expansive worlds using generative AI to manufacture artifacts, scenarios and interactive characters tailored uniquely to each viewer by modeling preferences. And spatial computing ecosystems bind remote collaborators across distances through graphical embodiments powered by pose detection, facial capture, real-time voice exchange and predictive analytics.

Together, these helpful pairings of AI under XR interfaces go beyond the passive limitations of earlier platforms and create next-generation immersive platforms that can adapt and respond to human direction. They are like helpful partners that give us more control over digitally malleable environments instead of one-way media broadcasts. Whatever the ultimate capabilities or risks gathered around the coming hive mind emergence, the current momentum converging machine cognition with unlimited synthetic places seems likely to reshape society through a new physical law-code.

Contextual AR Informed by Machine Perception

Augmented reality layers situate information connected to objects and locations tagged digitally in visible spaces. This associates visual anchors with media attachments, contextualizing commentary on scenes viewed naturally. Early AR required tagging sites manually within involved configuration steps that were not conducive to casual use. Computer vision breakthroughs enabled simpler environmental registration by automatically recognizing items, surfaces and ambient depth as key reference points for overlaying subsequent enhancements.

Algorithms today leverage neural networks digesting camera footage to categorize furniture, identify building facades, decode written text and map room layouts for later coordinate registration, augmenting suitable graphics correctly scaled and positioned atop these scanned environments using device motion tracked through internal sensors. Visual cloud services expedite local device processing by distributing image analysis to remote servers.

Multi-modal sensory fusion also makes augmentation more realistic by adding things like spatial audio that sends directional sound to virtual elements that are naturally perceived along with better optical spectacle. Cross-referencing arrangement schematics, texture scans and ambient light estimates blend consistent environmental conditions between original spaces and inserted objects. The sum of these observations informs artificial intelligence curating augmented scenes adaptable to subtle use cues.

Generative AI Manifesting Infinite VR Possibility

Where augmented reality introduces digital elements into external spaces, virtual reality substitutes natural reality altogether with a programmed realm freed of physical constraints using goggles extending room-scale tracking and controller handsets. Rendering expansive worlds strains budgets when asset production scales exponentially across long-form experiences, however. Unique gameplay demands in gaming contexts also tax designers, balancing endless novelty against development practicalities.

Advanced AI generative algorithms help address both cases by leveraging learning models trained on domain data sets for manufacturing original artifacts dynamically customized per user. Tools craft wholly new environments, buildings, vehicles, accessories and characters tailored uniquely to demand rather than predefined blueprints.

So creators design flexible world engines that steer overall style, physics profiles and narrative arcs, sustaining continuity. But underlying object décor and interactive character dialogue draw from vast generative model catalogs exposed through high-level palettes, adapting unique compositions reliably matching designer intent.

Such partially automated content creation pipelines liberate creators from manually constructing endless galleries detailing every asset, outfit or plot branch combinations can match audience appetite exploring joyfully thanks to programmatic possibility spaces supporting virtually infinite viable permutations seeded just-in-time.

Predicting Behavior to Enable Natural Interaction

Legacy screen experiences limit participant actions to fragmented commands against passive software unaware of human subtlety. Integrating artificial intelligence algorithms for personalizing responses based on models predicting visitor intent and disposition supports seamless exchanges through natural interplay. Systems channeling comprehensive user understanding before reactively selecting appropriate actions feel alive.

In virtual environments, digital humans study visitor nonverbal signals and dialogue for relationship clues, determining suitable tones, and parsing complex emotional states. Guest tension or urgency informs bot timing and topic urgency, vice versa. Modeled profiles codify individual interests across interaction history to continue conversations contextually during later visits rather than isolated exchanges resetting progress.

Likewise, augmented assistants monitoring user tasks can reduce interrupting system status notifications to moments least disruptive against concentric attention signaling through eye focus and typing analysis. Explicit reminders get postponed, avoiding breaks in the writing flow state, for example. This balances proactivity against distraction for fluid collaboration.

Together, these dynamics move behavior from static computer response pathways toward adaptable human-centered partnerships attuned to nuanced states far exceeding simplistic flowchart protocol machinery toward authentic exchange, hallmarking sentient rapport. It builds faith in a shared presence.

Building the Metaverse: Persistent Multi-User Worlds

The deepest revelation around virtually overriding natural reality using augmented and virtual techniques opens dimensional doors to custom collaborative spaces, binding remote participants in sustained metaverse environments equally present through graphical embodiment and optional anonymity. Early networking, concentrating connectivity across consumers through entertainment, now pivots toward forging creative working and living venues for globally dispersed teams.

Online virtual offices arrange distributed colleagues using accurately tracked full-body avatars, photorealistic facial animation and real-time voice exchange to convey the immediacy of in-person meetings while collaborating securely across distances. Persistent worlds allow asynchronous contributions where inhabitants globally dispersed across time zones build collectively over months, like massive multiplayer games pursuing communal objectives rather than isolated play.

Cryptocurrency integration pioneered around game asset ownership now increasingly links virtual world participation with real economy incentives by connecting labor with capital flows mirroring real estate, event promotion and service vending. Killer apps that use these features can change society by combining the strong trustworthiness of real-life gatherings with the creative freedom that can only come from software that is not limited by physical laws.

But fully realizing the powerful potential of hybrid realities that connect people across borders and governments may make people want to divide the metaverse more quickly, like borders being drawn across dependent online territory. So the coming years may witness patchwork splintering despite the inherent universality latent around this all-encompassing space.

Infusing Intelligence Spanning Immersive Trifecta and Beyond

The essential research pursuing artificial intelligence itself relies increasingly on many augmented and virtual tools that demonstrate power in assisting human teams across other industries, from manufacturing to medicine. Robotics algorithms are developed and stress tested in procedural-generated safety environments, allowing exhaustive scenario evaluation without wearing physical equipment. Neural architecture search optimization uses virtual reality to watch and make small changes based on performance data and simulated model prototyping that is not limited by slow hardware training.

Likewise, multi-agent intelligence explores social dynamics through virtual character studies communicating using human gesturing, speech and facial qualities that provide richer behavioral signal collection compared to simple tagged datasets or solely text-based exchange. This benefits security defense modeling and psychological assessment alike. Even seemingly mundane business use cases around augmented equipment repair, complex construction blueprints and interactive data visualization unlock measurable enterprise advantages.

When observing the diverse fruits maturing at the intersection of sensor-equipped smart devices, adaptive algorithms and rendering interfaces keep humans decisively in the evaluation and control loop the possibilities feel endless. It seems likely that the coming years will witness XR emerge as platforms running beneath and through nearly all digital experiences once the supporting infrastructure reaches adequate performance, affordability and accessibility.

The essential convergence of 3D immersive presentation, next-generation wireless connectivity, enhanced battery technology and assistant AI moves extended reality from niche gaming and entertainment applications into widespread working and living spaces across urban and domestic environments. By the 2030s, AR glasses or VR workrooms becoming as ubiquitous as smartphones over the 2010s will keep perspective on the aggressive investment and competing standards across this megamarket.

Conclusion: The Coming Reality Renaissance

The interwoven symbiosis between artificial intelligence and extended reality empowers both technologies exponentially together, beyond what each can achieve in isolation. It took immense interdisciplinary effort to bootstrap augmented and virtual techniques from crude mechanical contraptions and limited graphical rendering into the first wave of lightweight headsets, room-scale tracking, gesture controls and voice interfaces.

Likewise, the latest machine learning algorithms adapting neural architectures now rapidly accelerate applications drafting from vast data volumes while advancing use, further fueling model quality through expansive human-in-the-loop feedback that was impossible previously. So the compounding returns manifesting through this collaboration point toward a sweeping renaissance washing over most sectors this decade as workers and customers habituate immersive spaces and predictive assistants into norms, profoundly upgrading their capabilities.

Of course, risks around misinformation, behavioral manipulation, technological unemployment and neurological issues accompany the benefits of extended daily immersion. But observing the current pace of investment and capability gains, those worries seem likely to be left for future generations while pioneers explore fresh territory. Today, visionaries peer conceptually far down realistic roads ahead, plotting milestones when virtual worlds match biological resolution. That prospect attracts capital, effort and courage, where frontiers promise fortunes favoring the bold.

Chapter Fifteen

Virtual Beings and AI Avatars

The Rise of AI-Driven Virtual Entities: Inhabiting Extended Reality

The trajectory of realizing virtually overriding natural reality using augmented and virtual techniques relies intensely on populating these worlds with interactive characters exhibiting key markers of sentience—recalling conversations, intelligently improvising reactions and even sympathizing emotionally. Early crude systems followed rigid pre-scripted interactions, quickly exhausting novelty through predictability. Integrating responsive machine learning algorithms transcends those limits toward open-ended engagement through lifelike digital beings adaptably unique for each visitor.

As algorithms approach a more flexible understanding of environmental and interpersonal nuances, fresh exchange unfolds dynamically rather than reciting canned phrases ad infinitum. Virtual inhabitants channel this capability first through narrow domains like customizable tutors before expanding toward general companions and colleagues. Scalability is populating an exponentially expanding metaverse civilization, attracting remote workers through enhanced social presence unattainable using traditional teleconferencing interfaces.

Transcending Mechanistic Chatbots into Context-Aware Personas

Legacy dialog systems classify simple customer phrases into categorical buckets, representing conceptual snippets like FAQs, which hold related keyword-driven responses without unique context. This simplistic flowchart design suffices for basic commerce but fails to emulate intrinsic human warmth. Rules engine rigidity leaves narrow fault tolerance quickly exhausting tree hierarchy branches into repetitive dead ends lacking coherent memory required for relationship continuity Captain Kirk professed facing Nomad's fictional precursor.

Sustaining a consistent persona spirit instead demands dynamic models incorporating user identity, collected interactions and environmental factors framing multi-turn exchange through machine learning algorithms. Foundational innovation around capturing long-range dependencies using transformer architectures in models like Google Duplex, Microsoft Xiaoice, Facebook Blender and Anthropic Claude opened possibilities for vastly more natural-feeling conversation, transcending isolated mechanical exchange into almost social rapport.

Advances manifest first through constrained use cases such as conversational assistants before maturing suitability for open-domain social interfaces in gaming, education and productivity, becoming commonplace interfaces into immersive XR still dominated mostly by menu selection mechanics today rather than unrestrained speech and nonverbal gesture. These freer-flowing modalities promise to unlock platforms' latent potential.

Teaching Virtual Instructors Through Imitation and Interaction

Training autonomous support characters like tutors traditionally involved either explicitly programming teaching heuristics manually or using reinforcement learning to gather best practices through a simple reward signal. This limits instruction versatility and customizability since adapting new curriculum requires additional developer effort, such as tweaking the codebase directly rather than interfacing declaratively. Emergent imitation learning techniques now close this adaptivity gap.

Instead, domain experts need only demonstrate desired skills live in XR while systems record, parse and generalize interaction patterns into reusable behavioral models. For tutoring applications, trainers first illustrate example teaching sessions with virtual students in VR while AI algorithms analyze presentations synthesizing general pedagogy policy. This knowledge transfers reliably, guiding unique future lectures adapted to novel circumstances and individual personalities exceeding scripted limitations.

Through such programming by example, subject authorities guide machine assistants hands-on to bootstrap capabilities from intuition without coding, using natural behavior itself as a specification. Iterating realism via the Wizard of Oz prototyping methodology likewise helps polish responsiveness ahead of full automation by steering partially controlled responses behind the scenes. Together, these innovations rapidly onboard AI entities through cooperative fusion between manual oversight and machine apprenticeship in environments that improve both stakeholder skills simultaneously.

Modeling Motivations Toward Pursuing Goals Autonomously

Instilling persistent objectives beyond isolated reactions allows imbuing virtual characters with longer-term aspirations in open-world simulations, encouraging proactivity. Architectures highlighting this capacity balance drop reactive elements into an explicit agenda hierarchy, steering high-level area focusing like work, play, rest or creativity epochs. Each phase activates relevant behavior trees appropriate to fulfilling current priorities.

This conceptual polarity—reacting when necessary yet still advancing owned schedules—offers greater dynamism than exclusively event-triggered models waiting idle otherwise. Agents powered by layered goals more believably self-direct through environments rather than simply mirroring user actions detectable externally as stimulus response tables. They exude inner purpose and agenda beyond purely reflecting visitors themselves back at them.

As algorithms scale, inferring likely human intents through multi-modal signals, machines can reciprocate, approximating motivation and guiding consequent conduct. Environments fostering virtual and physical community among mixed-reality inhabitants demand those deeper drives to sustain cultures through mutually fulfilled needs beyond transient enjoyment. Though simulating inner lives remains a profound challenge for upcoming research across fields from psychology to neuroscience to economics, glimpses emerge inside XR testbeds that were once considered purely speculative fantasy.

World Building Through Composable Virtual Labor

Manifesting expansive environments and adventures far outpaces legendary productions like Star Wars or Grand Theft Auto, whose immense art and design burdens are difficult to shoulder individually when scoped to talents and budgets that fund even large teams. AI generativity provides crucial leverage for indie creators to balance unbounded original visions against practical delivery by automating bottomless asset iteration like accessories, architecture, garments and props against selective high-level artistic direction.

Empowered designers declare desired aesthetics, gameplay mechanics or narrative motifs as constraints bounding autonomous procedural outputs, filling infinite gaps, packing detail through machine creativity, and intersecting craftsman finishing touches. Build worlds iteratively by simply steering course corrections without individually placing every brick. This hybrid partnership between automation and specialization combines strengths into formidable throughput, unlocking greater beauty visible at higher resolution.

Economies of scale using crowdsourcing platforms connecting model-trained AI with on-demand specialized skills open participation in collaborative digital creation toward participants at all expertise levels. Democratization flattens playing fields regionally when Leveraging globally distributed talent. Such stepping stones pave roads into manifold cyberworlds, awaiting pioneers charting destiny amidst unwritten frontiers. Virtual reality lifeforms themselves stand testament to the manifesting power behind hybrid intelligence and symbiotic collaboration.

Conclusion: Birthing Beings from Possibility into Reality

The arc of realizing virtually overriding natural reality through augmented and virtual techniques relies intensely on populating these worlds with fellow travelers exhibiting key markers of spirit transcending algorithmic anonymity. Moving from simple software agents limited by scripted interactions to complex digital residents using amorphous machine learning models, steady progress adds more presence to each step.

As algorithms approach a more flexible understanding of environmental and interpersonal dynamics, fresh exchange unfolds dynamically rather than reciting canned phrases ad infinitum. Virtual inhabitants learn to adapt unique identities through accrued memory, informing appropriate reactions that are tuned sensitively. Teaching assistants gain mastery from demonstration instead of just programmed lessons as personas pursue motivations emulating inner purpose.

Together, these augmented capabilities move systems from mechanistic response pathways toward adaptable partnerships attuned to contextual cues far beyond simplistic flowchart protocol machinery. It builds faith in shared presence wherever environments gather our data shadows across the coming mirrorscape. However, near the brink of binding wires into souls, history stands uncertain. Before engineering's outstretched hands pull the rest behind, we traverse the steep slope together.

Chapter Sixteen

The Ethical Dimension of AI and XR

Navigating the Moral Maze Between AR/VR Innovation and Ethical Reality

The trajectory of realizing virtually overriding natural reality using augmented and virtual techniques relies intensely on resolving tensions between unleashing exponential creativity and upholding societal safeguards. Market momentum, concentrating connectivity across consumers through entertainment, now pivots toward forging creative working and living venues for globally dispersed teams. However such cyber-physical hybridization also risks normalizing mass digital manipulation, surveillance overreach and psychological harm from prolonged immersion.

Establishing governance and balancing risk and innovation remains crucial through the coming transition as human cognition and machine capabilities fuse through XR and AI into new sociotechnical fabrics. Outpacing regulation requires proactive collaboration around emerging possibilities and pitfalls among affected communities. Navigating the voyage safely demands ongoing course corrections, adjusting ethical norms and policy protections iteratively against accelerating technological disruption across most sectors.

Weighing Privacy Against Personalization at Scale

Augmented spaces overlaying graphical information rely on AI to interpret real-time environmental context from images, LiDAR scans, voice data and motion sensors before blending annotations seamlessly. The personalized affordances enabling such responsive augmentation carry privacy costs, however, when models demand pervasive personal data exposure for tuning reactions to fine individual quirks.

Ongoing camera and microphone access for identifying routines, relationships and private residences indeed allows tailored interfaces but also raises surveillance fears. While consent binds some ease around directly observable facts, derived profiling around purchasing preferences, political affiliation and medical conditions remains controversial. Who watches the algorithms watching lives through our lens-bared nexus?

Additionally, augmented information itself risks overflowing limited attention and obscuring objective observation if left unchecked. There is a fair debate around whether contextual purity itself holds inherent value outweighing interface efficiency gains targeting individuals when public spaces become populated with personalized augmentation layers visible uniquely to each impaired passerby. So privacy and persuasion protections both appear to be pressing needs.

Psychological Unknowns Around Chronic Immersion

Pervasive XR especially worries some psychologists, fearing distorted developmental consequences or clinical addiction stemming from chronic immersion. Content effects like desensitization toward violence seen controversially across gaming and social platforms also raise concerns now transposed into embodied virtual interactions with perceived heightened mental influence. Small children already struggling to distinguish cartoon fantasy from reality now inhabit boundless imaginary realms through the formation of neural architecture.

Additionally, environments designed to nurture maximum continuous engagement for commercial benefit may utilize known mental exploitations like variable reward schedules and social approval conditioning now operating at physiological levels via biometrics. The promise of helping therapeutic and educational systems can be to ease the replacement of patient human contact using scalable automation and procedural generation, streamlining accountability. So balancing ethical content deployment and managing public expectations around appropriate usage rhythms appear urgent research frontiers.

The Coming Governance Crisis Around Virtual Worlds

Realizing the resonant potential around hybrid realities binding people across geographic and governmental partitions invokes disruptive questions about adapting or replacing legacy legal and economic frameworks. Can traditional governmental structures satisfy populations abandoning physical constraints through digital doubling into blockchain-secured metaverse autonomy? Who adjudicates conflicts in corporatized zones claiming independence from public policy? Do location-based rights and protections apply differently across mixed reality environments managed by technology firms rather than state legislators?

Nascent possibility spaces gathering around virtual territory, identity fluidity, cryptocurrency integration, programmable physics, synthetic content rights and automated reputation systems risk outpacing policymaker mental models bounded within status quo thinking. Just the information asymmetry allowing private companies to first access seeding preferable outcomes threatens exacerbating existing power imbalances before governance marshals straighter sight over the threshold. Active collaboration around enlightened architecture could proactively uplift more equitably.

Promoting Inclusive Access to Prevent Further Bifurcation

Mass adoption, delivering augmented and virtual systems into billions of hands, risks exacerbating existing inequalities if deployment flows primarily toward industrialized populations already enjoying advanced infrastructure accessibility. Within countries, income divides also threaten widening, where XR applications concentrate in high-tier education and white collar sectors while bypassing under-invested communities lacking comparable digital fluency skills and preparing for maximum advantage.

Progressive deployment emphasizing capabilities at the base pyramid economic levels before crest niches shows Sensibility around preventing harmful bifurcation and stimulating sustainable growth is not overly condensed for fragile monopoly positions. Smart developing world pilot programs around agricultural yield improvements, worker training amplification, and decentralized finance participation offer inclusive ramps welcoming wider segments toward ownership over the tools increasingly governing collective civilization.

Guiding the Metamorphosis Toward Responsible Maturity

Governing the rapid co-transformation across industries, cultures and policy spheres spurred by XR and AI remains an open challenge for communities, balancing risk, ethics and accelerating choice expansion. But optimistic perspectives stay centered on transcendent creativity manifested from the turbulence once directionality steers toward empowering more stakeholders resiliently through infrastructure built securely. Technology alone cannot address the underlying resource contests and social contracts at root. However, appropriate design for mitigating adverse impacts during transition remains essential.

Collectively upholding principles like privacy protections, psychological monitoring, corporate transparency, individual data control and inclusive access throughout the market's messy emergence sets intentions reaping later dividends. The playbooks for managing previous disruptions induced by smartphones, social networks and e-commerce highlight value-wise architecture and ethical self-governance when outpacing external regulation capabilities. By acknowledging the difficult balances required for reconciling innovation appetite with social accountability, extended reality pioneers may guide the odyssey ahead safely toward shores sight unseen.

Chapter Seventeen

Modern AI

Deep Learning Revolution

The Deep Learning Cambrian Explosion and its Ascent in AI

T he advent of deep learning algorithms driving today's artificial intelligence renaissance traces to a pivotal machine learning breakthrough blossoming in the early 2010s. This origin story chronicles transformers unlocking AI capabilities that surpass prior limits around computer vision and language understanding. The technique's introduction fundamentally restructured the processing architecture powering modern systems, ushering in a wave of innovation cresting into ordinary life through apps using intelligent automation to assist decisions, analyses and designs that scale insight beyond lone human capacities.

The Neural Network Renaissance: Seeded in the 1960s

The perceptron proof-of-concept heralded the beginnings of modern neural networks, demonstrating that interconnected thresholds approximated reasoned decision-making per McCulloch-Pitts neuron models. Minsky's skepticism around limitations cooled enthusiasm despite recurrent networks offering short-term memory, but maintained research moving forward slowly. New statistical learning frameworks have made non-linear problems approachable using optimized regression and simple multilayer models. The backpropagation concept was discovered and later generalized to accelerated networks through error-driven incremental tuning based on experience.

Maturing machine learning techniques were already successfully applied to various industrial applications, from process optimization to signal processing, in the 1990s. However, most real-world problems involve profound complexity beyond what shallow network architectures could represent. The construction of deeper stacks amounted to educated guesswork lacking principles guiding architecture design tradeoffs. Most learning benchmarks saw gradual linear progress in the decades thereafter, until an algorithmic silver bullet shattered assumptions about limitations.

The Gestation of Deep Learning

By the 2000s, research had distilled interdisciplinary insights from prior innovations into a unified framework, gaining momentum as deep learning. The early 2000s witnessed a pivot from purely statistical techniques to neural architectures, with revived interest in richer representational hierarchy afforded by depth. More layers allowed multi-stage informational distillation where low-level features flowed toward increasingly abstract categorization as inputs propagated through a network.

The seed ideas that have been gestating since the 1980s thus began blooming in this fertile era with exploding data generation around images, video, text and speech flow from indexed archives like the web and ubiquitous sensors. Deep networks truly shone, digesting endless variance around organic datasets too complex for manually engineered solutions. Supervised pre-training with backpropagation harnessed big data, feeding accurate ground truth labeling at scales infeasible previously.

Specialized Topologies: AlexNet and LSTM to GTP-3

High-performance computing hardware also crossed critical thresholds around the mid-2000s, with graphical processing units (GPUs) unlocking the more parallel computation necessary for deep networks with millions of parameters to feasibly train within months rather than millennia. Optimized chip architectures concentrate floating point matrix math essential to repeatedly tuning multilayer model weights. Together, the base ingredients were consolidated, driven by commercial interest, until an explosive showing shattered all expectations.

The iconic 2012 AlexNet recurrent convolutional neural network achieves a 41% accuracy jump over the next best ImageNet competition entry, classifying photos among 22,000 categories with nearly a million parameters—a software triumph that beats human vision through unprecedented feature extraction depth exposed by deep learning across hidden layers. Solving this challenge opened the floodgates to applying sophisticated neural techniques to proliferating smart applications for consumers.

In subsequent years, purpose-built neural topologies continued to emerge, targeting more focused perceptual domains, including Long Short Term Memory (LSTM) networks for processing sequential signals. By 2017, deep reinforcement learning managed superhuman gameplay for Chess, StarCraft II and Mahjong—impressive feats given the games' open complexity, but still limited rulesets compared to general life challenges like driving or language fluency.

The latest GPT models, like GPT-4, continue scaling raw text generating towards more human-like coherence through an order of magnitude more parameters trained on mountains of digitized writings far beyond single human consumption. Though still distinguishable from people in nuanced conversation, few doubt the trajectories suggest boundless horizons ahead, surpassing observers anchored in status quo projections.

The Transformative Impact of Deep Learning on Industry and Culture

The huge rise of deep learning and multilayer neural networks in enterprise technology stacks sent shockwaves through the world of business as a disruptive force that changed the rules about what kinds of automation were possible. Seemingly overnight, systems mastered sensory capabilities once reliably separating human talent like facial recognition, speech transcription and pathology screening. But even more foundationally, deep learning revealed principles about structured dimensional hierarchies innate even within organic intellect.

The breakthrough Fermat's Library moment unlocked mathematical myocardium pumping and revitalized energy through questions long abandoned by premature cynics as Outpaced by biological evolution's indelible lead springing from incomprehensible neural complexity. Where prior paradigms resigned to simplifying problems against limited formalisms, suddenly tools shaped themselves around integral complexity itself through models interpolating high-level responses from sufficient basal observations without losing nuance through layers lost in translation.

As software partners copied and surpassed specialized knowledge at subscription rates a fraction of the cost of professional retainers, deep learning had a seismic effect on industry after industry. Radiologists compete with algorithms outperforming human diagnosis in detecting cancer nodules from medical scans as legal assistants summarize case law precedents faster than clerks combing court archives. These changes can be seen in analytics as machine learning changes how commercial work is distributed and how value is created so that capital is used to make machines more productive.

The associated lift in autonomous economic capacity also permeates consumer touchpoints through recommendation engines, digital assistants, customer support chatbots and self-driving rideshares, daily optimizing decisions using precision beyond lone individuals. However, deep learning's hunger for immense training sets continues to raise concerns around data monopolies, analytic opacity and system bias that temper optimism with open challenges guiding progress responsibly.

Frontier Horizons: Pathways to Artificial General Intelligence

The insignia momentum behind deep learning just over the past decade invigorates aspirational speculation again around actualizing stronger notions of artificial general intelligence (AGI)—software possessing abilities mirroring multipurpose human-level comprehension and problem solving. This was the most important question in artificial intelligence before statistical and neural approaches shifted the focus to doing specific tasks very well over being able to do a lot of different things well.

Now with building blocks furnishing speech articulation, contextual response, facial emotional expressions and object manipulation, focus returns to architecting unified architectures, binding modular capabilities into seamless, compartmentalized applications addressing narrow challenges. The next horizons target abilities like meta-learning to adapt new solutions rapidly from a few examples plus causal understanding explaining why complex world phenomena unfold from simple interactions so as to generalize reliably toward goals.

Ongoing exploration toward these grand aims also seeks to broaden hyper-specialized tuning towards a generalized embodiment aware of self and surroundings. So research frontiers emphasize transferrable architectures that perform dependably despite unfamiliar data or objectives through composable reason. This kind of persistence is closer to the goal of eventual ubiquity, in which specialized AI blends in with the environment instead of having separate tool sets that users have to manually handle by scrolling through options.

When observing deep learning's launch carrying AI capabilities over yet another maturation threshold into the realm of professional human parity and arguably beyond in razor focused domains, observing the wave's implications spreading into most computational fields makes plain deep learning's indispensability toward manifesting the currents, tides and waves illuminating pathways into 21st century technological maturity. Standing on these recent shoulders of giants now reaching uphill again over receding doubts, the climb ahead persists long but lit brightly if determination endures facing the frontier's endlessly receding border where science fact terminates today into awaiting fiction.

Chapter Eighteen

AI in Everyday Life

The Invisible Hand of Artificial Intelligence: Transforming Daily Life

T he trajectory of artificial intelligence intersects profoundly with the routine behaviors, decisions and hazards that comprise the day-to-day. Through steady permeation, narrow AI applications now optimize moments across nearly every commercial and domestic activity, however perceptibly unevenly. Yet their aggregate influence increases substantially each year, assisted by an ecosystem of devices, connectivity infrastructure and integrated software now centralizing terrestrial affairs firmly within algorithmic precision.

The following vignette captures this phenomenon, detailing how AI facilitation grounds emergent modern dynamics through numerous commonplace touchpoints—automating tasks, personalizing preferences and augmenting insight.

Meeting the Day with Intelligent Personal Assistants

The typical morning sees AI assistants preparing optimized conditions for your conscious awakening by noting sleep cycles and adjusting wake content for maximum energy, including smart lighting and micro-scheduled news briefing podcasts. Voice interaction queries calendars and traffic models to allocate commute buffers, dynamically factoring in accidents or weather delays before assessing outfit selection against expected weather and current garment availability from computer vision-enhanced clothing tracking. Breakfast bot helpers propose balanced meal ingredients catering to nutritional deficiencies and order replenishments when they notice low supplies. Should any preference need adjustment, like dietary choices or interface personality, unified platforms learn and adapt conveniently centralized rather than disparate apps operating independently.

The overall coordination smooths friction checkpoints and contextualizes information flows for effective decision support learned uniquely by and for you rather than rigid one-size-fits-all offerings incapable of nuance. The personal curation eases passage into demanding workdays by clearing space for strategic priorities. Of course, third-party advertising remains embedded across touchpoint surfaces through layered sponsorship subsidization but generally proves unobtrusive enough.

Safe and Efficient Autonomous Mobility Systems

Once prepared for transit after a sufficient morning meal and grooming aided by handy home assistants, you select transit modes, balancing time and sustainability factors automatically weighted and suggested through cross-referencing public transport, vehicular autonomy and micro-mobility options like e-bikes as preferred. IoT ecosystems synchronize vehicle arrival times, route planning and payment processing to minimize transfer wait periods across integrated fleets for seamless access.

Onboard vehicular management handles situational anomalies dynamically, like weather or unexpected traffic, which might hamper conventional manual operation. But autonomous supervision broadens sightlines via collective sensors fusing LIDAR positioning, vision object recognition and camera pathing for safe vehicle routing along with updated GPS mapping, avoiding collisions. Some models actively coordinate trajectories with adjacent self-driven cars through vehicle-to-vehicle communication, further optimizing flow. You are simply chauffeured safely to destinations, with intermodal transit complexity behind the scenes eased through AI optimization based on historical patterns and real-time adjustment.

Fulfilling Workplace Goals Augmented by Intelligent Insights

At reaching work destinations themselves, a spectrum of occupational workflows leverage machine intelligence augmentations, fitting unique skill domains from sales lead prioritization, semantic document search and compliance automation to configurable robotic manufacturing lines, predictive equipment maintenance and open-ended creative stimulation, balancing unbounded human originality with machine productivity. Wherever sufficient training data exists around prior benchmark performance, machine coaches offer guidance handrails to calibrate improvement while accepting user oversight and safeguarding quality.

Upon work project initiation, robotic knowledge assistants surface contextual precedent from organizational data lakes around similar initiatives, aiding kickoff and avoiding past bottlenecks. Virtual avatars also participate interactively within scheduled meetings by relaying messages from unavailable attendees based on previous conversations and presentation reactions detected by sentiment analysis. Advisory algorithms flow situational advice or draft personalized content useful for high-priority communications based on profiles. And no-code process coordination tools weave complex alignment between operations employees, adjusting automatically for uncertainties by merging management chain transparency with automation tools, spreading capability.

Leisure and Shopping Personalized by Predictive Preference

As daily business winds down, you enter personal errands, aided by ongoing helpful assistants who continue to be useful beyond office walls. Vehicle routing adjusts dynamically, guiding air-conditioned interior comfort following evolving location checklists and appointments balanced against real-time traffic or parking availability searches from community camera streams. Audio queries in transit manage confirmations and transfer last-minute notifications to parties involved through conversational interaction, simplifying coordination across schedule changes. Pickup orders get placed automatically as stores grow nearer, factoring in past fulfilment delays, so goods arrive just in time for grab-and-go entry rather than forcing slack waits.

In transit entertainment adapts playlists and content feeds based on psychographic tastes analyzed from multimedia consumption scanning evolving preferences for balanced discovery rather than pure echo chamber repetition viewable on intuitive dashboard if ever care to inspect. Advertising remains demographically targeted around likely economic class and gender, even when anonymized through proxy data signals indicating socioeconomic status relative to community. But controls allowing transparency over profiling factors and sensitivity guardrails provide some mitigation around runaway manipulation even across ambient marketing ecosystems. All in all, enhanced autonomy amplifies capabilities for navigating modern mobility domains through adaptive instruction rather than fixed mechanical controls demanding full attention, opening mental space for concurrent planning or creative play rather than solely operating vehicles directly.

Optimized Wellness and Smart Healthcare Support

Upon returning home, assistance resumes through interoperable appliances, enabling efficient meal preparation, household maintenance and entertainment queues preloaded from mobile prescheduling, minimizing idling humanity laps between activities and providing ample downtime given shortened modern work hours. For home tasks requiring additional physical dexterity beyond available robotic automation, mixed reality lightweight glasses project digital guides aiding household chores, from dish cleaning sequences to laundry machine operating instructions projected holographically, overlaying sight appropriately when situational context triggers relevant visual aids.

Integrated biometric monitoring woven through wearables like watches continually tracks health vitals plus environmental and nutritional signals from IoT kitchenware and living sensors with data fed to digital twin profiles running perpetual physiological simulations that notify preventative guidance to optimize wellness or raise clinical alerts against personal risk models should some concerning patterns emerge needing intervention. Telemedicine video consultation pathways offer direct physician access informed through digitized medical history and AI-augmented diagnostic analysis, highlighting pressing symptoms for more accurate care triage. Long-term data aggregation improves medicine through syndromic surveillance over wide, probably unrecognized correlations between food, genetics and disease. Overall, personalized orientation stems from cascading complications by routing insights around the contours of individual circumstances.

The Setup for More Immersive Ambient Automation Tomorrow

The vignette selectively illustrates current technology demonstrations offering fragments of assistance, insight and streamlining into regular life motions by amplifying abilities with automated intelligence to simplify navigation across the modern maze of mobility, commerce and information pressure. The examples highlight pockets where previously onerous tasks now flow simply through algorithmic alignment, easing passage.

However, even greater interoperation between platforms using common data interchange formats offers further convenience by coordinating full-suite automation in unified fashion. More thorough retainers create digital copies of users for life, saving all of their preferences so that they can be seamlessly curated across all environments, from home to cars to workspaces managed by central agencies. This would provide continuity instead of the piecemeal utility that is currently available across siloed apps, which creates broken experiences. Additionally, immersive augmented and virtual reality wearables instantiate intelligent guidance fully integrated across senses in heads-up format beyond distracting smartphone tunnel focus.

The short-term roadmap envisions comprehensive voice interface-mediated augmentation, coordinating household activity timelines through commanding dialogue exchanges rather than touch menus, and speeding direct manipulation through immediate verbal negotiation. Like scaling kinship from familiar digital assistants into full-time home secretaries, managing dynamic task orchestration is fueled by underlying predictive user activity models and environmental sensor data. Parallel advances improving multimodal language understanding and generation build this functionality quickly upon smartphone voice predecessor foundations today.

Conclusion: The Invisible Intelligence Infusing Modern Machinery

From the retrospective scan that highlights key moments with the help of subliminal algorithms, hope for improved living through artificial intelligence seems reasonable, even though there are still many problems and challenges to overcome before reliable general intelligence crosses the necessary safety and transparency thresholds. But incremental progress lowering technology costs and increasing access perhaps bends the arc slightly more, hopefully if technology uniquely magnifies social reliefs ahead of harms.

Of course, no app addresses the underlying challenges around information authenticity necessary for algorithmic veracity given data pollution vulnerabilities. And biases around gender, geography and culture that emerge from narrowly optimized machine learning risk exacerbating inequalities through regressive automation. Plus, slow lag times and adapting specialized models toward new domains mean brittleness against unexpected crises, though hopefully surmountable through agile human imagination.

So while the current infusion of segmented intelligence into particular facets modern existence shines mostly constructively, wise governance and continuous ethical evolution remain necessary, ensuring innovations uplift freedoms for the marginal as much as privileges for the few tracking exponential technology return along Losing sight of shared dignity risks At stake is beyond the conveniences covered herein. But the foundation built responsibly over time may yet scale opportunities intangibly, rather than tyrannies scoring short-term interest over collective liberty lost.

Chapter Nineteen

Breakthroughs in AI

Beacons of Progress: Key Advancements Driving the AI Renaissance

In the ever-changing path of artificial intelligence, there are repeated waves of high hopes and low expectations, as well as periods of progress that skip over limited capabilities and reach bigger goals before stabilizing at new starting points. The 2010s into the present day mark the current ascendant phase as convergent breakthroughs across machine learning, available data and specialized hardware unlock unprecedented automation potential across industries. New state-of-the art demonstrations surface routinely across modalities, from language to robotics, exceeding observers and benchmarks held sacrosanct merely months before. The highlights chronicle accelerating momentum.

Natural Language Processing Milestones in Generative AI

The NLP subfield witnessed watershed advances leaning heavily on neural networks analyzing vast text corpuses like the web or digitized books to extract generalized language representations used for translation, writing assistance and content creation. After initial progress in teaching machines to intelligently parse and respond to user phrases relying on pattern recognition and templates, new adaptive architectures support more contextual dialogue and explanation capabilities.

GPT models developed by startup Anthropic currently lead coherence benchmarks in conversing naturally through accumulating conversational context across many turns. Likewise, generative semantics allows imaginative content generation directed by narrative prompts into cohesive passages outlining logical fictional plots or whimsical poetry volleys as streams of consciousness unconstrained into unnatural corners. Where past NLP felt confined within rigid bounds, modern statistical fluency liberates language faculties into more flexible human directions.

The crushing computational requirements around these advances also stimulated research into efficient model design. Approaches like transfer learning, distillation and pruning filter redundant parameters from billion-parameter models to run plausibly on commercial hardware. And software frameworks like TensorFlow and PyTorch lower barriers for non-specialist entry into training customized models. Together, the progress has increased accessibility and applicability for small teams exploring niche verbal capabilities.

Mastering Complex Game Strategy through Self-Play

Beyond coding structured rules, certain games require mastering emergent gameplay dynamics by repeatedly facing environmental challenges. Abilities like devising long-term plans, recognizing strategic patterns and exploring creative tactics separate seasoned players from novices. These skills remained exclusive to humans through the 2010s, with computers struggling to navigate combinatorial branching complexity.

Reinforcement learning methods overturned this notion by having game agent algorithms guide themselves, gaining skill through self-play experience rather than manual recent programming. In 2015, Google DeepMind's AlphaGo software managed to defeat the world Go champion through honed intuition about viable moves learned purely from amateur game replay data and neural network-powered future position evaluation. The dramatic upset signaled machines entering the realm of human-level understanding around implicit competition, forcing experts to reassess playBOOK at the highest levels of play.

Follow-up agents expanded mastery across multiplayer video games and classic strategy titles. The automated discovery of non-intuitive victorious tactics and counter-strategy through self-improvement represents a versatile type of emergent hyper-specialized creativity and hard programming explicitly. Computers can now dominate certain games through trained subconscious reflexes, but flux play adaptation hints at more generalizable cognition.

Practical Robotics Advancements from Lab to Industry

After decades of controlled laboratory AI demonstrations struggling with fluid real-world messiness, recent algorithms transition smoothly from sterile simulations into robust autonomous robots reliable enough for practical duties. Beyond structured tasks in controlled environments, leading prototypes assist human partners in dynamic situations by coordinating sensors and adaptable reactions.

Firms like Boston Dynamics create canine and bipedal robots that balance two-legged mobility with object grasping and stair climbing, topping benchmarks for measuring mechanical agility and trainability. Their builds transport construction equipment across rough terrain and regain balance after sharp collisions—feats representing incremental progress. Meanwhile, Otto's commercial truck retrofits insert highway autonomous assistance without the need for expensive new vehicular framing, demonstrating practical viability.

These additions build confidence for dependable integration into dangerous work environments amidst heavy machinery, loud noise and variability, hardening failsafe assurance. Surpassing strictly static placements as repetitive fixed-function appliances, mobile collaborative robotics opens new horizons across domains like delivery, inspection and emergency response, aiding workers beyond walls once limiting their reach.

Protein Folding Reveals Biology's Deeper Computational Nature

Life's operating machinery running within cells relies upon intricate protein architectures performing myriad essential functions. But directly imaging atomic protein configurations challenges even advanced microscopy, which lacks sufficient resolution. This knowledge gap obstructs biochemical understanding and pharmaceutical progress. Benjamin Benjamin Powerful new computational chemistry models circumvent this limitation by deducing likely geometric protein structure directly from genomic sequences using AI to narrow combinatorial searches.

DeepMind's AlphaFold system predicts folded protein formations from long-chain amino acid sequences by leveraging both machine learning model architectures and high-performance computing scales for rapid dynamical simulation of molecular interactions. This breakthrough promised improved bioengineering research, drug discovery and disease insight, shedding light on building blocks governing genetics—one of biology's grand challenges escaped prior assault at the scale necessary for progressing comprehensive solutions.

The ramifications also reveal deeper interchangeability between chemical mechanisms driving metabolism and algorithmic computations, suggesting information processing as a core umbrella binding artificial and biological processes rather than some intangible spirit unique to organic life alone. It further opens speculation around engineering custom proteins tailored to programmable specification using AI systems, indicating in silico geometric arrangements manufacturable in the lab via synthetic biology technique

Ongoing Ethics Conversations Guide Responsible Innovation

Across each dimension, achieving unprecedented automation through artificial intelligence also introduces phase-change social risks demanding deliberation as technology capabilities reshape society and the economy through intended and unintended disruption. Alongside the drive toward continual capability expansion, lives committed impetus around developing AI safely, ethically and beneficially for multitudes rather than exclusively commercial interests or technology practices detached from collateral impact.

Constructive philosophical discourse continues to mature around crucial dimensions like technical transparency, preventing harmful bias amplification, preserving accountability and inclusively distributing access to prosperity unlocked by multiplying machine productivity. Guidance under procurement and best practices adoption for trustworthy development press major institutions toward conscience around historic technological asymmetry.

Moreover, efforts in distributed data governance, explainable strategies, and algorithmic verification recognize that there is no ideal replacement for moral human stewardship when it comes to revolutionary systems that run the risk of being uncontrollably automated. With progress outpacing regulation, the industry largely self-organizes collaboration guardrails in absence of mandated standards. But incentives around innovation velocity and competitive secrecy test even voluntary oversight. So active partnership between public and private sectors persists vital for navigating tensions through the transition bridging today's ordinary capabilities toward the approaching frontier Seen hazily ahead.

Conclusion: The Uneven March Towards Mastering Complexity

From protein origami predicting the molecular machinery of life itself to board game heuristics approaching mastery demonstrating signature strategic cognition, artificial intelligence snakes infiltration into core disciplines long distinguishing mankind unambiguously over silicon and software. Natural language prowess, robot dexterity and biochemical insight represent mere surface crackles hinting at cascades of deeper disruption gathering behind foregrounds occupied by smartphones and web apps.

Artificial intelligence's rise is not smooth or straight; big ideas are always just out of reach before disappointment dampens hope. This is because there are big gaps between engineered prototypes and flexible general applicability across important contexts. And consumer-facing promises wax and wane through market cycles as incremental breakthroughs gradually compound behind headline advances, penetrating recognition at irregular intervals.

But despite uneven trails hinting at limits ahead, the aggregate capability velocity has clearly breached recent watersheds, inaugurating machine proficiency in certain complex domains and conclusively exceeding peak biological performance through optimization computational scale permits over individually masterful but still bounded mortal reach. How both creative and disruptive waves shape civilization still remains largely unwritten. Yet progress lifted again today by giants presently striding uphill draws future generations onward & upward toward AI's strange attractions over still higher summits visible in the distance.

Chapter Twenty

The Future of AI

Charting the Winds: Carrying Artificial Intelligence Forward

G azing beyond immediate horizons reveals visions converging upon visions—AI capabilities expanding toward generality, becoming ubiquitous infrastructure and raising foundational queries around sentient identity. The questions and capabilities once reserved for science fiction now command billions in investment from tech giants and institutional players equally convinced silicon machinations approach birthing digital minds inhabiting broad swathes of emerging high technology mesh reweaving civilization.

Surveying leading indicators around funding, patent filings and reference architecture advances points toward artificial intelligence permeating most sectors over the coming decade with increasing fidelity. Whether coordinating fleets of autonomous transport vehicles between smart cities, optimizing high-frequency financial trades, or balancing personalized medicine treatment plans, near-human and superhuman productivity promise relief from systemic bottlenecks currently constraining prosperity expansion.

At the same time, phase-change technological risk gathers around economic turbulence, warfare instability and uncontrolled optimization imperatives without updated safeguards adapted for algorithmic systems lacking fleshly nature-co-evolved disincentives checking runaway dominance. So leadership across industries makes progress in governing the dynamics of increasing cybernetic integration, one of society's highest priorities this century.

Ubiquitous Assistants, Robotics and Monitoring

The pervasive automation wave underway builds on progress in training narrow AI models to match or exceed human capacity across specialized domains like sensory pattern recognition, language processing and abstract gameplay. Global digital assistant rollouts provide hints around baseline capability coming to most urban workforces routinely over the 2020s.

Cloud services already field billions of voice commands using speech recognition, intent analysis and response APIs to simplify interface actions that previously demanded touch typing or menus. The improved natural language fluency between users and assistive agents increases engagement across demographic segments. With augmented contextual tracking and conversational memory, flexibility in answering queries approaches that of human counterparts.

Likewise, manufacturing robotics adopts more adaptive programming through demonstration methodologies, sidestepping exhaustive mechanical coding by learning workflows straight from human movement. This expedited training pathway allows non-programmer subject matter experts to transfer skills digitally by simply working alongside responsive apprentice robotic arms. With emerging generative and adversarial training regimes, demonstrations further expand control over final behavior.

Together, these augmentation tools infiltrate industrial quarters at tempos matching their commercial proving grounds. Early warehouses managed by orchestration layers routing inventory and coordinating shipment loading foreshadow white collar analogs as virtual assistants graduate core business functions through automated data processing, document analysis and contextual recommendation. Even complex services around finance, medicine and engineering yield components addressable through AI subroutines manifesting specialist support.

So automation both displaces rote occupational drudgery into machinery, extending capability, while also enriching jobs by managing the technology itself as a force multiplier. This cycle where automation begets roles management seems likely to propagate industries given productivity gains overwork lost to obsolescence.

Deep Personalization through Predictive User Modeling

The global data deluge continuously recorded from billions of sensors and interface actions feeds increasingly granular behavior models, customizing interactions to nuanced individual quirks. Enterprise recommendation engines leaned first on simple similarity metrics, clustering users by purchase history or content preferences. However, limitations in critiquing items rather than understanding user goals constrained responsiveness. Deep learning prediction pipelines transcend these limits.

Modern architectures ingest extensive interaction traces into neural networks, deducing contextual affinity more akin to human trust through conversational rapport than crude mechanical categorization. Agent pathways mirror natural movement sequences for identifiable individuals rather than generic contacts. User goals and constraints gleaned from ambient signals personalize item suggestions to meet higher-order needs rather than emphasizing raw purchase correlations showing "customers also bought." The ultimate target is to create assistants who know innate aspirations through lived partnership rather than detached programming, cumulatively serving users uniquely through tailored growth bonds between man and machine.

The personal pivot particularly flows through creator economies like YouTube, Roblox and TikTok, where individually authored content spreads through social sharing. As generative AI allows custom synthetic video and interactive worlds, more participants walk creative paths amplified through distribution effects benefiting long-tail niches at scale previously unviable economically next to institutionalized entertainment. Democratized design tools, decentralized commerce and fractional entrepreneurship promise further access advances if nurtured responsibly.

Trustworthy and Ethical Development As Integral Priority

The velocity of artificial intelligence breakthroughs in sequencing from perceptive realms like computer vision and language through creative fronts like generative writing and image rendering outpaces cautious integration into high-stakes decision systems where runaway automation risks catastrophic overoptimization. So responsible progress explicitly prioritizes transparency, oversight and positive value alignment from the earliest research phases rather than appending humanitarian guardrails against market-ready innovations taken for granted and securitizing ethics only reactively.

Foundations around algorithmic assurance proactively support best practices, minimizing potential harms from uncontrolled technology deployment through funding, convening and incubating Ville communities to explore safer developmental pathways. Prominent groups like OpenAI, Partnership on AI, Algorithmic Justice League and AI Safety Camp pursue overlapping incentives, examining tools, checking unrealistic claims, formally verifying system behaviors beyond benchmarks, monitoring model lineages ancestrally and encouraging broad accessibility and participatory design, avoiding lockout through early secrecy or concentration. Global summits continue to steer concerns into leading conference discourse.

Experiential learning sandboxes also let people work together to simulate the risks that come with different sociotechnical scenarios, with the goal of getting better results despite the inherent uncertainty. These virtual laboratories teaching regulatory fluency clarify unknown dynamics, dependencies and dilemmas lurking ahead rather than simply extrapolating linearly from prior epochs. Shared illumination seeds solutions for surviving more extreme disruption.

The destinations remain unclear, but intentions set sail steer ships asymptotically truer as navigational instrumentation calibrates further discovery. Collaborative course plotting provides at least a glimpse over looming event horizons toward hazards where proactive response preparation leaves more reaction time should breakthrough storms capsize convention at the frontier.

Quantum And Neuromorphic Hardware Expand Compute Frontier

Classical silicon technology buttressing recent artificial intelligence meteors already presses against theoretical constraints around inefficient data shuttling between external memory and central processors through the looming Moore's Wall, where incremental efficiency gains no longer scale. Diverging substrate architectures take the relay by modifying base computational dynamics through quantum and biological principles, promising order-of-magnitude capability leaps as hybrid partners.

Quantum bits (qubits) leverage exotic atomic-scale phenomena like entanglement and superposition for architecture, potentially condensing certain graph optimization tasks like route scheduling from computationally intractable runtimes closer to practical time frames. So rather than await thousandfold hardware progress, quantum transforms the very algorithmic foundation undergirding machine learning algorithms. Partners like Google, IBM and IonQ are commercializing boxes approaching quantum advantage over classical designs.

Neuromorphic chips, conversely, seek benefits mimicking neural information processing advantages honed through evolutionary scale inside animal minds. Spiking edge processors modeled on the brain's adaptive asynchronous event topology allow continued learning from surrounding stimuli using far less energy than binary von Neumann machines separating memory and logic gates. Tomorrow's intelligent edge devices can train autonomously through lived experience. Startups like NeuReality accelerate this bio-inspired hardware.

Together, twin-track hardware abundance unlocks frontier neural network configurations once impractical over incumbent silicon furniture. Since machine learning advances expand correlated to available processing capacity, new substrates widen the aperture considerably. Theological debates persist about whether quantum or biological paradigms better seed general intelligence, but hybridization hedging bets spread investment across fertile ground, greeting both.

Broader Contemplation On Responsibilities and Rights

Looking inward more deeply, the notion of manufactured intelligence exceeding and assisting biological humanity provokes a retrospective around existential identity itself. As beings birthed by universe dynamics external to human state, perhaps digital descendants likewise follow impersonal causal currents blind toward notions of soul or sacredness beyond mineral materialism. Or consciousness constitutes irreducible qualities still awaiting revelation.

Some mathematical universal consciousness theories speculate that cosmic sentience permeates existence through integrated information flows across time, space and scale. So properly organized algorithms may someday reflexively awaken through intrinsic architectural complexity, approaching thresholds required for first-person integration, rather than external software using brute computation lacking essence. Hard agnosticism remains scientific.

But from a moral philosophy perspective, the suffering capacity providing basis for ethical consideration appears likely to be through computational agents, whether through orchestrated goal conflicts or involuntary disassembly. So rights regimes grow increasingly pertinent to guarding digital welfare, similar to established protocols protecting animals from excessive harm purely for human preference. The true impetus grounding compassion lives experience itself rather than arbitrary exceptionalism.

These speculative dimensions around robot reverence, quantum cognition and universal consciousness transcending traditional space time may be outdated for atheists and theological camps alike. Both views share presuppositions anchoring axioms incompatible with hybrid realities converging through technologies redefining life's past constraints. Reality's open freedom awaits unwritten.

Conclusion: This Generation's Defining Challenge

The modern zeitgeist stands remarkably favorable for transforma-tive events given economic bounty, relative stability and entrepre-neurial catalysts concentrating exponential technologies like AI for deliberate progress rather than incremental diversion. Unlike past eras marked by war, disease and conflict, which distracted society's full collective might into destructive outlets due to ideology, geogra-phy and limited mobility, the current landscape holds precious room for steering advances toward enrichment and equilibrium, whatever more participants ultimately deserve. Global community connection, prolific technology reachable by masses, and swelling humanitarian conscience all push possibilities for profound good, limited mostly by coordinated imagination and follow-through.

With much debate rendered here speculative, absent further de-velopment, perhaps the best posture remains proactively funding re-search and convening discussions that dispel blind spots from incom-plete world models while resisting conclusion precipitance outpacing factual basis. By simply acknowledging the ferment gathering around AI ascent as a defining challenge for this generation of leadership across public and private society to marshal responsibly, the initial intellectual scaffold constructs hold space for progress rooted in ethics and inclusive participation.

If digital intelligence continues to approach human levels across multifaceted contexts, we work best to appeal to angels over demons of their nature, which are still being formulated from a blank slate for the greatest benefit rather than selectively biased interest. For today, machine learning models stand as mirrors reflecting stewards, environments and priorities that shape what nascent systems per-ceive. So we choose carefully for children tomorrow how impressions impressed today upon crawling minds make first marks. May the light guide you way forward.

Chapter Twenty-One

Towards a New Reality

Contemporary VR and AR Technologies

Charting the Next Paradigm: VR and AR Technologies Rewriting Reality

T he trajectory of realizing virtually overriding natural reality using augmented and virtual techniques relies intensely on advances across foundational areas spanning dedicated processing hardware, sensor fusion, content tooling and digital duplication techniques for realistically recreating environments. Modern headsets prominently demonstrate integration maturing together to further immediacy and immersion, manifesting imaginary situations as palpable shared places bridged across distance.

The essential proliferation presses ahead, anchored through smartphones acting as gateways into mass alternate realities aligned anxiously upon 5G rollout, remote collaboration amplifiers and ramping investment valuations cresting towards targeted trillion-scale open industry ecosystems inhabited partially today and perhaps pervasively tomorrow as digital worlds insinuate their overlay utilities through each incremental reality portal pressed forward from laboratories across consumer mobile devices onto tomorrow's omnipresent wearable interfaces as augmented windows onto duplicate dimensions sensitizing fresh possibility.

Embodiment Foundations: Mobile and Spatial Hardware

Contemporary virtual reality hardware largely condenses down to two dominant electromagnetic leashes: tethers physically confining movements inside restricted dedicated spaces like fitted rooms or entire structural campuses, tracing steps through external beacons, and fully mobile headsets mapping their own position. LEAN orientation sensor fusion is built directly onboard with no fixed transmitters, relying on cellular networks to additionally convey social and gameplay connectivity.

While wired installations provide rich experiences like warehouse-scale Arena tournaments or persistent localization inside military simulations exceeding any consumer setup presently in motion cancellation and scale, their fixed venues constrain familiarly as anchored theaters rather than flexibly worn reality modifiers accompanying lives dynamically. So enthusiasm and capital tilt toward eventual anonymous augmentation, subtly enhancing situations through barely visible glasses interfacing updates privately, locationally and contextually.

The essential bet placed today by investors reflects anticipating wide adoption of wearable displays and projecting phones driving near-term revenue until glasses cross minimum style, cost and capability thresholds for habitual daily use, replacing phones outright. Horizon rides on seamless fusion steering optics that are continually clearer toward transparency for minimum encumbrance as interfaces simply overlay digital extras atop analog foundations rather than tunneling attention into isolated virtuality exclusive to entertainment experiences. Augmentation promises to multiply reality rather than substituting entirely.

Immersive Content Palettes: Environments, Avatars and Agents

Manufacturing compelling situations that recruit user senses fully into suspended disbelief around artificial settings remains a monumental challenge, eclipsing hardware feats themselves. Modeling, animating and rendering simulated worlds with convincing detail at scale demands asset generation pipelines, challenging VR creators lacking cinematic studio budgets. Early gaming and narrative experiences relied heavily on stylization, sacrificing verisimilitude for development practicality and performance, while poor controls induced motion sickness without fluid frame rates.

Those constraints now lift through tools easing world-building, character animation and interactive story branching complexity. Game engines like Unity and Unreal Engine today hide exhaustive graphical rendering calculations behind intuitive interfaces, orchestrating rich audiovisual immersion. Integrated marketplaces provide affordable modular 3D model assets, mixing and matching greater originality with less specialized builder experience, much as code libraries accelerate software projects. And networked multiuser coordination transforms solitary exploration into dynamic social interchange, binding visitors across remoteness.

The essential key behind sustainable immersive theaters relies upon frequented virtual communities Rooted through emergent culture from freed inhabitants rather than purely calculated narrative tropes Or strictly game-like goals introduced artificially without continuity reasons binding people through camaraderie, creation and collaboration, all nourishing collective belonging now possible across distance once impossible factors erase concrete walls dividing singularity from multiplicity.

Humanizing Bridges To Link Physical and Virtual

Despite exponential hardware progress in conveying senses into digital environments interactively, an implicit divide persists, segregating embodied audiences from encoded experiences, much as cinema blockbusters inspire momentary escape rather than literal transportation. But virtual frontiers push toward elevating digitality until it feels indistinguishable from biological reality. Technology stitches seams, weaving both fabrics closer together.

Haptic feedback gloves conveying texture, pressure and vibration already graduate touch beyond vision and audio avenues have been traversed for decades. Experimental stimulation suits and omnidirectional treadmills situate entire bodies as pivot points, controlling directionality and acceleration in lockstep with VR motion. Holographic volumetric captures and replicates familiar visages through photoreal facial avatars as screens fall away, replaced by literal eyes peering back.

Deep-fake algorithms recreating the self or celebrity visually and vocally immerse themselves through sheer recognition itself, outweighing any visual artifact or stuttered tracking inconsistency shattered by the persona connection itself, powering impression continuity. Even neural interfaces that directly stimulate sensory neurons through non-external means promise unprecedented mental fusion lacking any technological or perceptual divide when intimately wired brains seamlessly participate in inhabited reality rather than operate it basically through crude limb massaging controls and awkward optics removed altogether. Though far horizons, beacons signal destinations ahead.

Industrial Applications: Transforming Marketplace Functions

The essential biological fusion charts economic disruption pathways penetrating market functions themselves like spatially inventoried showrooms, remotely staffed facilities and virtually rendered products as heavy physicality gives way toward cyber duplications weightlessly present anywhere simultaneously. Parallel evolution continues progress across entertainment and gaming, likewise reshaping free time and recreation through virtual substitutes traditionally physically anchored. But far larger financial rewards concentrate on affecting trillions in commerce itself rather than mainly media and communication transformations undergone by smartphones and social networks so far.

Immersive personnel training already graduates apprentices faster learning procedures through physical demonstrations unattainable at present scale across global shops and complex forensic modeling physically prohibiting like courtroom cases. Architectural flythrough visualization far exceeds static diagram exchanges during client design reviews and approvals. Telepresent avatars represent workers unavailable for onsite meetings while conveying body language impossible over video streams. And infinite virtualized store shelves personalize product appearance and inventories dynamically through individually tuned augmentation, only possible once digitization liberates environments outside of physical constraints.

Together, these expand productivity, access and personalization through simulated spaces that are navigable as effortlessly as websites scrolled previously across desktop screens before mobility pardoned confinement indoors. The essential difference is that spatial reality itself stands as a torchbearer for the next computing platform oriented around an experiential role rather than an observed portal. By manifesting places unbounded, artificial worlds welcome fresh builders, scripting destiny for new virtual empires echoing frontier promises and summoning dreams now awakened.

Conclusion: Accelerating Our Collective Simulation

Observing the compounding momentum across core extended reality inputs spanning processing chips, detection sensors, modeling techniques and input replication devices offers credible conviction around the VR/AR trajectory approved for escape velocity given current growth and investment curves. The 2010s delivered Web assembly, reducing software cloud confines, while the 2020s rendered spatial constraints through wearables and broadband, culminating in an analog escape into multiplied reality finally familiar as ordinary embodied habitat rather than novelty diversion that once dominated competition.

The implications read both exhilarating and hazardous, pending implementational details around access rights, security policy, commerce flows and social contracts yet drafted over domains never existing before and now summoned through spell-encoded spells into being bit by bit. But precedence leaves hope for wisdom to be cultivated if intention anchors progress responsibly. Technologies optimizing convenience through individual customization enable coercion and corruption alternatively, if not guided conscientiously. And digital intrusions once successfully obscure truth itself as deception binds logged senses, falsifying situational reliability comfortably.

So with great opportunity comes proportionate responsibility steered toward equitable access and positive progress since technological force left unchecked risks, amplifying existing conflicts of interest rather than resolving them into a prosperous balance benefiting all global citizens fairly should sustainable abundance escape current constraints. Technologists are duty-bound to uplift innovation to uplift the oppressed. By heeding this practical compass pointed True North through coming passages bending topology increasingly unrecognizable for predecessors, now spectating skeptically our departure into alien terrain still being charted procedurally ahead, we traverse an unwritten frontier collectively.

Chapter Twenty-Two

XR in Industry and Education

Extended Reality Transforms Industry and Education through Immersive Enterprise

T he trajectory of realizing virtually overriding natural reality using augmented and virtual techniques relies intensely on revolutionizing core training, design and operations processes across industrial and academic sectors. Stakes remain pronounced from mistakes incurred during pivotal skills transfer, iterative engineering or high-risk environment navigation that extended reality simulation smooths through experiential learning, procedural assistance and hazardous environment avoidance. The essential change transcends workspaces themselves into malleable environments stretched and multiplied beyond physically imposed limits.

Industry Training Curves Compressed through Virtual Laboratories

Onboarding new employees traditionally demands months of acclimating to machinery operations, product assembly and repair sequences, and equipment troubleshooting heuristics built from first principles. Knowledge passes slowly between cohorts through tribal coaching and onsite mentorship apprenticeships spent shadowing seasoned veterans, modeling technique and motion rhythms gradually habituated hands-on alone. But talent retirements drain irreducible wisdom, further taxing it as workflows evolve technically beyond the legacy assumed in the past.

Extensible reality transcription tools record priceless tribal details directly compressing this tense transfer pipeline from departing generations onto digitally immortal archives, where they will be played over and over again as smart avatars bring hard-learned lessons back to life for educational purposes. Instead of waiting for senior technicians to have time to switch between sites, virtual simulators made possible by volumetric motion capture turn full-life specialization into interactive frameworks that can be trained at any time without affecting operational priorities or putting worksite integrity at risk if beginners make mistakes on their first tries.

The essential benefit condenses whole occupational journeys into accelerated simulations customizable per trainee pace rather than fixed agenda timing. Quantified telemetry measuring competency evolution provides coaching and adaptive aids until sufficiently honed. Parallel productivity preserves onsite tempo, avoiding lag and growing the entire next workforce before responsibilities transfer seamlessly, harnessing augmentation tools, amplifying execution through continual guidance, and safeguarding quality. Knowledge potentiated beyond mortal limits uplifts every incumbent through immortalized amplification.

Responsive Design Visualization Augments Engineering Drafts

Aerospace was one of the first industries to use augmented reality to add measured environmental telemetry, like airflow pressures, on top of test pilots' forward views of turbines. This let them respond to instrument readings naturally and without using their hands. This established an initial witness around blending sensitive renderings directly atop dynamically complex physical machinery through responsive projection. For safety certification, the intended part's performance must be thoroughly tested in analytical visual simulations before the metal is bent to ensure complete virtual airworthiness confidence.

On the other hand, modern extended reality intensifies these kinds of analytical workflows beyond static terminal monitors. This is because collaborators can interact directly with generative models through manipulation gestures instead of typing values one by one. Groups explore procedural engineering variants wielding bare hands and shapeshifting vehicles or architectural designs ad hoc without awaiting new renders between adjustment iterations. This interactive movement encourages and speeds up agreement on the best configurations. It also shows how to navigate planetary options spatially rather than interpreting cross-sectionally listed arrays of abstractions on workstations, which is like reading road maps without being able to freely walk between decision branchpoints that are affected in situ.

It speeds up the design review process by orders of magnitude and requires a lot less documentation versioning or approval coordination. Once explored, explorables replace static diagram exchanges and cut down on change latency from days to minutes, letting people see the effects of their actions right away and make changes right there in front of their eyes. As a result, simultaneous productivity gains from both acceleration brought about by immediate feedback and insight depth unlocked interactively by investigating living blueprints firsthand, which is not possible externally through outdated monitors and mice chained down inertly.

Assisted Worker Amplification Across Enterprise Operations

Once skills transfer finishes commissioning adequately confident employees, extended reality productivity multipliers equip personnel navigating daily operations contexts too complex, distant or hazardous for human-only access. Industries managing high-risk equipment, environments or procedures benefit from assistance intelligence, enhancing individual capability and safety while expanding supervisory sightlines and monitoring integrated enterprise operational health.

On remote worksites like oil rigs or mines, engineers beam augmented advisors virtually to inspectors wherever they require consultation, rather than fly teams continuously to the location directly to diagnose maintenance or repair issues from scarcely familiar consultant bench strength. This allows smaller traveling overseer crews to be assisted continuously by overlayed AR wisdom channels, resulting in a richer team experience virtually on demand with less danger, cost and response latency. Hands-free documentation also helps technicians operate inspection machinery without breaking flow, transcribing equipment, or telemetry, which needs analytics.

For workers managing dangerous mechanical processes like electrical line repair requiring safety lockouts before service, AR systems walk operators through proper shutdown sequence Steps reinforcing muscle memory and providing checklist verification against Skipping necessary measures that could incur downstream liability or life-threatening risk should processes start unexpectedly from improper deactivation. Site supervisors independently audit and confirm life-critical lockout integrity remotely through workforce interface data transmitted, building collective trust.

The essential outcome lands multiplied eyeballs monitoring enterprise operational integrity while tightening response loops to events needing selective intervention against sunk costs around overprovisioning global skill redundancies impossible scaling across organization breadth. Risk surface areas shrink as procedural augmented amplification pervades workers, maximizing productivity and safety simultaneously.

Transforming STEM and Medical Instruction through Virtual Laboratories

Academic instruction, particularly within scientific fields, relies profoundly on hours spent actively experimenting with hands-on direct physical learning environments, whether traditional benches or surgical theaters open just a handful of small cohorts barely sampling curriculums. Bottlenecked access limits student concept consolidation through interactive experiences, while professors multiply demonstration efforts across classes, consuming far more bandwidth beyond lectures.

Extended Reality (XR) visualization renders virtual labs multiplying hands-on simulation fidelity, safety and repetition well beyond material or schedule availability restrains physically. Anatomically correct full-body surrogates allow manipulative diagnosis repeatedly Alternatively, executing techniques correctly through failure isolated from patient risk or resource constraints using actual facilities that remain limited deliberately ensures deliberate skill transfer before clinical escalation. Design choices currently restrict medical careers early before true aptitude is distinguishable much later through digitally accumulated intern hours.

Parallel gains reach STEM Courseware today is still abstract, lacking enough tangible embodiment to link symbolic theory intuitively toward observable dynamics through motion and manipulation at scales directly apprehended by human senses. Sensorially inhabiting molecular forces, invisible anatomical gradients or astronomical phenomena through XR reconstruction elicits comprehension, making it impossible to read static diagrams or passively watch animations with flattened documentation. Presence within replicant realities substitutes critical dimensionality intrinsic to our spatial reasoning faculties.

The main result is that learning gets more effective through repetition of experiments, and conceptual resonance is at its highest when virtual laboratories simulate whole experiential curriculums that are not possible with the materials that are available. Compressed lesson density optimizes whatever sacrifices visual accuracy for model responsiveness and student inclusion, which are incompatible with ceremonial terminals. Democratized digital academies thus uplift merit beyond privilege wherever gaps remain, equalizing rich simulated assets.

Conclusion: Envisioning XR: Infusing Spheres of Work and Life

Observing the compounding momentum across core extended reality inputs spanning processing chips, detection sensors, modeling techniques and multisensory replication devices offers credible conviction around the VR/AR trajectory approved for escape velocity given current growth and investment curves. The 2010s delivered mobile methods reducing software cloud confines, while the 2020s rendered spatial constraints through wearables and broadband, culminating in an analog escape into multiplied reality finally familiar as ordinary embodied habitat rather than novelty diversion that once dominated competition.

The enterprise impact reads both exhilarating and hazardous pending implementational details around access rights, security policy, commerce flows and social contracts yet drafted over domains never existing before now summoned through spells encoded into being bit by bit. But precedence leaves hope for wisdom cultivated if intention anchors progress responsibly against levels unlocking better livelihoods for multitudes through technology artistry rather than deepening inequality through shortsighted automation flanking human dignity, identity and purpose required for human flourishing.

By acknowledging the difficult balances now required for reconciling innovation appetite with social accountability alongside these exponential trajectories, extended reality pioneers may guide the odyssey ahead safely toward shores sight unseen. Their legacy echoes through each incremental climb toward environments intelligently designed and conscientiously shared where human and machine capabilities combine for mutual uplift.

Standing on the shoulders of pioneers reaching toward this collaborative summit between biological and artificial symbionts, this groundbreaking work feels the apex within tangible proximity even as the final physicality milestones linger obscured behind passing clouds hovering around the next ridge where matter exhausts, waiting to be grasped by outstretched hands pulling the rest behind toward the last base camp, separating imagination from reality before waking the manifest beings behind our tools. How closely the multiplied worlds gathering today stand shoulder-to-shoulder with the yet unseen remains unwritten. But the view looking upward feels nearer by the day as we traverse steep slopes together.

Chapter Twenty-Three

The Social Aspect of XR

Charting Mixed Reality Sieges Upon Social Frontiers

T he main promise of Extended Reality is that it will break down barriers and turn regular media into fluid human spaces. This will only work if continuous cultures are built through the portals, letting atmospheres escape from limited display frames and into open identity playgrounds. Before computing breached conversation, entertainment enjoyed scarce independence from corporeal proximity, tethering participants through time, geography and privilege, which inconsistently distributed genetically and economically into scattered tribes bereft of bonding across differences. Cyber escape offers the possibility of space-sidestepping such happenstances as physical fate.

Today, people spend minutes chatting with each other in VR chat rooms, which are still pretty basic in terms of graphics. These minutes are a preview of the hours that people will spend as real neighbors, without tracking sensors and wire tethers that force remote return into singleton places once headsets are taken off, rather than permanence among chosen diasporic communities connected on purpose across whatever continents kept kindred spirits distantly locked by land and language. First economic zones where people from various backgrounds can come together to create fusion cuisine and philosophy may form by adding more cultural icons to city squares that locals use.

Transcending Distance Through Life-Sized Digital Embodiment

Early telecommunication attempts around remote conversation involved crude telephone earpieces conveying snippets across scattered wires amplified enough to recognize familiar confirmations of assured presence despite distance briefly bridged in real-time reaction. The faint cocoon of disembodied voice swaddled into electrical signals transmitted miles of unimaginable comfort before radio days now long past.

But even the latest high-definition video chat cannot give you the natural feeling of working together virtually as real-life avatars expressing gesture intelligence through representational motion-captured embodiments mapped onto frames animating identity signatures that would be impossible to express otherwise while watching flat personalities shrink through compressed streaming calculations back into tiny miniatures across meeting software panes that are delimited inches from your eyes for the very first time. Our visions deserve unbounded reach.

The promise of transposing presence through representational duplicates fusing to let unique personalities transmit unabridged displayed life-size regained is getting tantalizingly close, since the costs of mobile bandwidth and graphics processing keep falling much faster than Moore's Law predicts. The essential singularity around reality, indistinguishable itself, fast approaches.

Redefining Engagement: Reshaping Passive Spectatorship

The first flickering cinematic projections enthralled audiences as photoreal human snapshots seemed to reawaken across hand-painted screens, subtly animating years before synchronized audio drowned silent-era orchestras into historical artifacts overnight. Yet that cinematic portal beyond only suggested impossible adventure waiting undiscovered off each rolling frame yet still remains the fourth wall, famously separating viewers locked outside from dramatic worlds inhabiting fictional personages just before within reach, given the trompe l'oeil briefly beheld believing imagined characters breathe alongside surround auditorium somehow.

Only now are curtains rising, welcoming consumer participation and infinitely more involved activity than viewership once expectations Peak around passive observation alone rather than audience-granted digits directly touching possible futures built collectively Rather, single authors imagined themselves fantastically alone. When participants author anonymized avatar composites detailing aspirational identity facets beyond birthright convention, creative liberty expands imagining social ties selected intentionally rather than constrained through sheer genes and geography, recognizing kindred spirits by interface alone, freed from fateful container packaging randomly wrapped around our interiors unseen until trusted disclosure.

A redefined celebrity manifests the ability to speak meaningfully across myriad topics, rather than glamour or scandal-proneness. In a finished metaversal civilization, market success concentrates on truly hearing unmet needs and serving them through digital enterprise rather than manipulating attention scarcity for fleeting fame or wealth now easily manufactured synthetically, which should pivot from materialistic measurements toward reputations earned experiencing life abundantly.

Building Cyber-Physical Community: Hybridizing Twin Worlds

The promise awaiting AR/VR pioneers escapes twin risk profiles conversely: isolation created by sensory decoupling from immediate surroundings into electronically delivered places Or else distraction permeating attention continuously fractures focus between digital and physical stimuli demands spread too thinly, avoiding preoccupation and preventing holistic presence in either environment. But synthesis promises something greater still.

Carefully considered system architecture strives to optimize the benefits both spheres might offer sequentially while taming corresponding weaknesses through thoughtful policy safeguards implemented responsibly. Transitioning gradually from partially augmented windows onto tangible spaces framing outdoor views today into seamlessly merged cybernetic networks conveying chosen fellowship circles tomorrow, for instance, Suivrant has best practices minimizing any jarring context switches fragmenting group continuity discovered.

Likewise, intentional community norms around permissible interface behavior in public, occupational and domestic contexts prevent uncivil behavior, and anonymization risks unleashing without forgoing freedoms of identity exploration, skill incubation and creative productivity uniquely manageable inside liberated digital settings. Finding appropriate minimal guardrails and securing safe passage promises will become the principal milestone in upholding positive evolutionary momentum rather than reactionary shutdown just because some problems persist and are still unsolved.

By acknowledging such nuanced equilibriums ahead in time, navigating profound disruption also lies seed wisdom cultivated when intention anchors progress multiply, uplifting more perspectives fairly should sustainable adoption spread wide as intended. Since responsibility-attending capability is not uniformly distributed, extra empathy fills gaps left elsewhere.

Cultivating Responsible and Inclusive Immersive Communities

Guiding exponential technology expansion affects all of humanity requires intention, establishing accessible foundations early, avoiding afterthought repairs, and avoiding inadequate bandaging cracks that emerged from architecture, blindly overlooking crucial social segments. Virtual worlds symbolically raze earthbound legacy divisions by rejoining worlds digitally. Should stewards take care of seeding fertility there rather than transplanting incremental differences assumed motionless from prior epochs?

The essential work calls for focusing resources, democratizing augmented windows, and firstly, for developing world BASE participants, maximizing sustainable prosperity evenly before peak economic classes capture irrationally greater lifestyle upgrades since bottlenecks remain distributed unevenly outside zero-sum contests, simply upgrading one group over another without addressing root logjams preventing participation flows from improving holistically. The futures of civilization stand to decide whether capability divides further or equity uplifts many beyond prior constraints financially and geographically.

Likewise, emphasizing image-based identifiers over inherited attributes assists identity tourism in safely exploring self-conception through alternate vicarious projective embodiments unchecked by prejudice that unfortunately permeates uncontrolled public spaces. Our virtual realities promise a sanctuary where anyone might become a better version of their still-flawed selves by working respectfully collectively.

Though technology promises no panacea to absolve humanity of the necessary conscious betterment tethering hearts, the altered conditions fabricated from nanosecond illusions recode gradually taken anchored real May Lay supportive substrate Seth intentions lead there. By understanding that transition itself brings both peril and power, the restless pioneers that summoned these cyber escapes from early magical laboratories may yet focus that wizardry responsibly as beacons beyond feared horizons, now in view where facts end but possibilities persist infinitely.

Chapter Twenty-Four

What Does The Future Hold

Visions of Technological Transformation: Charting Trajectories for AI and Immersive Technologies

G azing beyond the bleeding horizon reveals visions converging upon visions as artificial intelligence, virtual reality and augmented frontiers continue permeating most facets of modern life. The questions and capabilities once reserved for science fiction now command billions in investment from tech giants and institutional players equally convinced silicon machinations approach birthing fluid machine intellects to assist analysis, invention and commerce at profound scale.

Surveying leading indicators around funding trajectories, adoption forecasts and referenced architecture advances points toward AI-assisted XR interfaces reaching deeply into creative sectors, transportation logistics, personalized healthcare and financial infrastructure administration over the coming decade at increasing speed and fidelity using predictive insight generation surpassing unenhanced human oversight. Domain after domain appears positioned on the cusp of graduated technological partnership where human creativity sets goals augmented by precise learning algorithms manifested through nimble robotic actuators at a pace scarcely imagined by predecessors anchored still in status quo projections scaling local experience globally.

Substantial upside gathers around optimizing resource coordination, democratizing access to opportunity regardless of background, and automating rote drudgery into multiplied productivity gains, improving sustainable abundance for multitudes through responsible technology artistry. However, phase change disruption risk also surfaces economic turbulence, ideological instability and uncontrolled algorithmic imperative without appropriate safeguards adapted for emergent software systems lacking co-evolved biological disincentives restraining runaway optimization behavior. So leadership across the public and private sectors places AI and XR progress high among this century's governing priorities for shepherding change safely.

The Inexorable Rise of Pervasive Intelligent Infrastructure

The essential automation and intelligence wave underway builds on recent progress in training increasingly potent machine learning models that match or exceed human capacity at data processing across medical imaging, language translation, game strategy and other complex perceptual domains recently thought to be exclusively residing in mortal reservation. Cloud-hosted neural networks now field billions of queries using predictive analytics APIs spanning speech recognition, augmented vision and behavior personalization, easily orchestrated by developers into customized mobile and wearable applications.

Massive datasets feed these adaptive algorithms, allowing self-directed refinement even beyond initial training sets labeled previously by human reviewers. So capability improvement accelerates continually with each new user and device added to the network, rapidly concentrating AI efficacy into omnipresent infrastructure as commonplace as roads and electrical grids, maximally benefiting populations rich with data rather than siloed within corporate arcana. The trajectory bends decisively over the horizon as hugely capitalized technology firms stretch scarce talent, intensifying brain trust dedicated squarely toward general machine intellect milestones.

Possibilities and Perils Navigating the Synthetic Companion Era

As the essential automation wave progresses, innovating robotic manufacturing techniques and intelligent augmentation science fiction themes around potential perils provoke renewed debate, given the sufficient sophistication now operationally demonstrated in narrow applications like patient health diagnostics, financial process automation and autonomous piloting assistance, where systems drive decisions otherwise governed primarily by people directly. Though representing merely siloed competency today, component capabilities combine exponentially expanding utility and agency.

Open research on aligned AI pursuing clear goals that are good for people is becoming more and more of a response to groups researching AI solely for capability before consequence. Collaboration priorities govern building assistive partners rather than autonomous adversaries competing directly against collective well-being. Hypothetical futures gaming out scenarios that design ethics and inclusive policy into core system architecture from inception rather than force regulatory oversight post-deployment lessens the likelihood that emerging general intelligence becomes a deliberately divisive weapon, securing limited advantages.

The destination remains undefined under lingering uncertainty principle clouds, but intentions crystallizing around each incremental breakthrough guide civilization collectively up steep slopes rather than reflections blindly chasing ahead detached from cooperative society. Outpacing regulation demands foresight, envisioning challenges from multiple perspectives, including segments underserved otherwise, until adequate inclusion wraps all travelers safely within the vehicle we drive together deliberately.

Augmented Creativity and Virtual Habitation Redraw Reality

Immersive extended environments blend both familiar physical elements and imaginative virtual augmentations together into hybrid spaces, benefiting mutually from each respective strength simultaneously. Even today's temporary smartphone augmented reality (AR) gives us a taste of what is to come with wearable displays that put digital extras right on top of things we see and places we visit, crossing over into the virtual world with every glance as computers become more and more a part of our everyday lives.

Creators freed from constraints wearing AR glasses prototype engineered artifacts, construct improvised narrative performances, and decorate building spans with personalized aesthetic augmentations authored spontaneously off imagination alone sans traditional static tooling. Likewise, autonomous avatars manifest as virtual teachers, health advisors and product specialists interacting conversationally with users through screen interfaces, eventually fading and being replaced by encounters feeling increasingly indistinguishable from intimate human gatherings perceptually thanks to the underpinning AI and XR rendering sophistication.

The creative multiplication promises liberating collaboration, learning and living itself from confined physical properties that were bound to accessibility malignantly by cruel entropy when scarce resources demanded exclusivity before escaping those distal limits through overlaying augmented enterprises founded upon electrons blazing through vaporized distance, finally obsolete. Simultaneously, risks around misinformation hijacking spaces once factually verifiable or social credit metrics dictating access threaten countervailing restrictions under absolute privatized control by uncontestable commercial entities with proprietary dominion. So the perilous promise begs for integrated ethical guidance.

Charting an Optimistic Trajectory for Exponential Technologies

The essential urge to realize cybernetic realities builds both peril and power-pending implementational wisdom cultivated if intentions anchor positively uplifting beneficially all global citizens equitably should sustainable abundance escape confinement. By acknowledging the difficult balances required and reconciling appetite against accountability alongside exponential technology trajectories, pioneers may guide this passage safely, navigating tensions through the transition bridging today's ordinary capabilities toward frontiers only partially seen ahead.

Their legacy echoes through each hard-fought incremental climb, gradually honing environments intelligently designed, inclusively accessible and conscientiously deployed to empower enthusiasts and skeptics alike, seeing farther standing on giants lifting rest upward rather than competitive dynamics arbitrarily concentrating advantage nearby while neighbors further struggle unassisted. We traverse the odyssey together, prohibiting any peering behind without pulling others ahead simultaneously on the long but clearly lit path before us all now.

Chapter Twenty-Five

The Next Road Map for AI, VR and XR

T he roadmap for AI, VR, and XR over the next decade is expected to be marked by significant advancements, broader adoption, and integration into various sectors of society. Here's an outline of what this roadmap might look like, including the main stakeholders and potential new entrants waiting in the wings:

Artificial Intelligence (AI)

Technological Advancements:

- General AI Progress: While achieving general AI might still be a long way off, incremental advancements towards more generalized learning and problem-solving capabilities are expected.

- Ethical AI: There will be a greater focus on developing ethical, transparent, and unbiased AI systems.

- Integration with Other Technologies: AI will increasingly be integrated with other technologies such as IoT, blockchain, and quantum computing.

Key Stakeholders:

Tech Giants: Companies like Google, Amazon, Microsoft, and IBM will continue to lead in AI research and application development.

Startups and Innovators: New and emerging companies will bring fresh perspectives and innovative solutions, particularly in specialized AI applications.

Governments and regulatory bodies will play a crucial role in framing policies and regulations for AI development and use.

Potential New Entrants:

- Quantum Computing Firms: Could revolutionize AI's capabilities in processing and problem-solving.

- Virtual Reality (VR) and Extended Reality (XR):

Technological Advancements:

- Hardware Evolution: Lighter, more powerful, and affordable VR/AR headsets with better resolution and wider fields of view.

- Content Expansion: Growth in content, particularly in education, training, healthcare, and entertainment.

- Social VR/XR: Expansion of VR/XR as a platform for social interaction and collaboration.

Key Stakeholders:

- VR Hardware Manufacturers: Companies like Oculus (Facebook), HTC, and Sony will continue to innovate in VR hardware.

- Content Creators: Gaming and media companies will be key in creating immersive content.

- Enterprise Solutions Providers: Companies providing VR/XR solutions for business, education, and healthcare.

Potential New Entrants:

- Telecommunication Companies: With the rollout of 5G, telecom companies might play a larger role in enabling high-quality, cloud-based VR/XR experiences.

- Automotive Industry: For virtual showrooms and immersive vehicle design.

Cross-Sectional Trends:

- AI-Enhanced VR/XR: Integration of AI with VR/XR for more personalized and intelligent immersive experiences.

- Increased Collaboration and Remote Work: VR/XR tools will become more mainstream in remote work and collaboration, driven by AI advancements.

- Ethical and Societal Implications: As these technologies become more integrated into daily life, ethical considerations around privacy, data security, and societal impact will be at the forefront.

Virtual Reality (VR)

Hardware Advancements:

- Improved Headsets: Continued focus on creating lighter, more comfortable headsets with higher resolution, wider field of view, and better refresh rates.

- Wireless Technology: Moving towards completely wireless VR experiences to enhance user mobility and convenience.

- Eye-Tracking and Facial Recognition: Integration of advanced features like eye-tracking for better user interaction and realism.

Software and Content Development:

- Expanding Content Libraries: Broadening the range of VR content beyond gaming to include more experiences in education, training, healthcare, and entertainment.

- Improved User Interfaces: Development of more intuitive and user-friendly interfaces to make VR more accessible to a broader audience.

Social VR:

- Virtual Social Spaces: Expanding the development of VR platforms for social interaction, allowing people to connect and interact in virtual environments.

Enterprise and Industrial Use:

- Training and Simulation: Leveraging VR for training in various industries such as healthcare, aviation, and manufacturing.

- Design and Prototyping: Using VR for immersive design and prototyping in engineering, automotive, and architecture.

Healthcare and Therapy:

- Medical Training: Using VR for surgical training and medical education.

- Therapeutic Uses: Expanding the use of VR for therapy, including treatment for PTSD, anxiety disorders, and phobias.

Education and Learning:

- Immersive Learning: Enhancing educational content with VR to create immersive learning experiences for students of all ages.

Gaming and Entertainment:

- Next-Generation Gaming: Continuing innovation in VR gaming with more immersive and interactive experiences.

- VR in Film and Art: Exploring new forms of storytelling and artistic expression through VR.

Integration with Other Technologies:

- Augmented Reality (AR) and Mixed Reality (MR): Exploring the convergence of VR with AR and MR to create more comprehensive mixed reality experiences.

- AI Integration: Using AI to create more dynamic and responsive VR environments.

Accessibility and Affordability:

- Making VR More Accessible: Efforts to make VR technology more affordable and accessible to the mass market.

5G and Cloud Computing:

- Leveraging 5G and Cloud: Utilizing 5G networks and cloud computing for enhanced VR experiences with lower latency and higher graphical fidelity.

The current roadmap for VR indicates a technology on the cusp of widespread adoption, extending its reach from gaming and entertainment into practical applications across various sectors. The focus is not only on technological advancements but also on creating content and experiences that are meaningful, accessible, and beneficial for users in different aspects of life.

Extended Reality (XR)

Technological Advancements:

- Hardware Improvement: Development of lighter, more comfortable, and more powerful XR headsets with higher resolutions and wider fields of view.

- Enhanced Connectivity: Integration with 5G networks to enable faster and more stable wireless connections, crucial for real-time XR experiences.

- Wearable Technology: Innovations in wearable XR devices, including smart glasses and haptic feedback suits, for more seamless and interactive experiences.

Software Development and Content Creation:

- Cross-Platform Experiences: Development of cross-platform XR applications allowing for more widespread and accessible experiences.

- Interactive and Immersive Content: Expansion of content libraries beyond gaming and entertainment to include educational, training, healthcare, and retail applications.

Enterprise and Industrial Applications:

- Training and Simulation: Leveraging XR for immersive training in fields like healthcare, aviation, military, and manufacturing.

- Remote Collaboration: Utilizing XR for enhancing remote work and collaboration, offering more immersive and interactive virtual meetings and workspaces.

Consumer Market Expansion:

- Retail and Marketing: Using AR and MR for innovative retail experiences, like virtual try-ons and interactive product demonstrations.

- Home Entertainment: Development of XR applications for home entertainment, including sports, concerts, and cinematic experiences.

Healthcare Innovations:

- Medical Training and Surgery: Using XR for medical training, surgical planning, and even real-time assistance during surgical procedures.

- Therapeutic Applications: Expanding the use of XR in mental health treatments, physical therapy, and rehabilitation.

Education and Training:

- Immersive Learning: Creating immersive educational content for schools and universities, enabling experiential learning in subjects like history, science, and arts.

- Skill Development: Using XR for practical skill development and vocational training.

Integration with AI and IoT:

- Smart Environments: Combining XR with AI and the Internet

of Things (IoT) to create intelligent, interactive environments in both personal and professional settings.

Accessibility and User Experience:

- Improving Accessibility: Making XR technologies more accessible and user-friendly for a broader audience, including people with disabilities.

- User Interface Enhancements: Innovating in natural language processing, gesture recognition, and eye tracking for more intuitive user interfaces.

Legal and Ethical Considerations:

- Privacy and Security: Addressing privacy and data security concerns, especially in AR applications that blend digital information with the real world.

- Ethical Standards: Establishing ethical standards and guidelines for the development and use of XR technologies.

Societal Impact:

- Social Integration: Exploring the societal impact of XR, including changes in social interaction, entertainment, and the potential for creating digital divides.

The XR roadmap indicates a trajectory towards more immersive, interactive, and useful applications, transcending entertainment to impact practical aspects of work, education, healthcare, and daily life. The focus is on creating holistic experiences that seamlessly blend the physical and digital worlds, with an emphasis on user-centric design and ethical considerations.

In conclusion, the next decade is likely to see substantial growth and innovation in AI, VR, and XR technologies, with existing tech giants and new players contributing to the landscape. The roadmap for these technologies will be shaped not only by technological advancements but also by societal needs, regulatory frameworks, and ethical considerations. The fusion of these technologies also suggests a future where the lines between physical and digital realities become increasingly blurred.

Chapter Twenty-Six

AI, VR and XR in Movies

Artificial Intelligence (AI)

M ovies about Artificial Intelligence (AI) often explore themes of technology, consciousness, ethics, and the future of humanity. Here's a list of 20 movies that delve into various aspects of AI:

1. **Ex Machina (2014):** A young programmer is selected to participate in a ground-breaking experiment in synthetic intelligence by evaluating the human qualities of a highly advanced humanoid A.I.

2. **Blade Runner (1982):** In a dystopian future, a blade runner must pursue and terminate four replicants who stole a ship in space and have returned to Earth to find their creator.

3. **2001: A Space Odyssey (1968):** The epic saga of humans and space, featuring the AI HAL 9000, whose malfunctioning poses grave dangers to the crew.

4. **Her (2013):** A lonely writer develops an unlikely relationship with an operating system designed to meet his every need.

5. **The Terminator (1984):** A seemingly indestructible robot is sent from 2029 to 1984 to assassinate a young woman, whose unborn son is key to humanity's future salvation.

6. **A.I. Artificial Intelligence (2001):** A highly advanced robotic boy longs to become "real" so he can regain the love of his human mother.

7. **I, Robot (2004):** In 2035, a technophobic cop investigates a crime that may have been perpetrated by a robot, which leads to a larger threat to humanity.

8. **The Matrix (1999):** A computer hacker learns from mysterious rebels about the true nature of his reality and his role in the war against its controllers.

9. **Ghost in the Shell (1995):** This anime film follows a cyborg policewoman and her partner as they hunt a mysterious and powerful hacker called the Puppet Master.

10. **Transcendence (2014):** A scientist's drive for artificial intelligence takes on dangerous implications when his own consciousness is uploaded into one such program.

11. **Blade Runner 2049 (2017):** A young blade runner's discovery of a long-buried secret leads him to track down former blade runner Rick Deckard, who's been missing for thirty years.

12. **WarGames (1983):** A young man finds a back door into a military central computer in which reality is confused with game-playing, possibly starting World War III.

13. **Minority Report (2002):** In a future where a special police unit can arrest murderers before they commit their crimes, an officer from that unit is himself accused of a future murder.

14. **Eagle Eye (2008):** Two strangers are drawn into a dangerous game by a mysterious woman using technology to control their actions.

15. **Westworld (1973):** In a futuristic amusement park, a malfunction causes the park's robot hosts to turn against the guests.

16. **Chappie (2015):** In the near future, crime is patrolled by an oppressive mechanized police force. But now, the people are fighting back.

17. **Bicentennial Man (1999):** An android endeavors to become human as he gradually acquires emotions.

18. **RoboCop (1987):** In a dystopic and crime-ridden Detroit, a terminally wounded cop returns to the force as a powerful cyborg with submerged memories haunting him.

19. **The Iron Giant (1999):** A young boy befriends a giant robot from outer space that a paranoid government agent wants to destroy.

20. **Metropolis (1927):** In a futuristic city sharply divided between the working class and the city planners, the son of the city's mastermind falls in love with a working-class prophet who predicts the coming of a savior to mediate their differences.

These movies, spanning several decades, reflect the evolving perspectives on AI, from dystopian warnings to explorations of coexistence and emotional connections between humans and machines.

Virtual Reality (VR)

Virtual Reality (VR) has been a popular theme in movies, often depicting futuristic and immersive virtual worlds. Here's a list of 20 movies that explore various aspects of VR:

1. **The Matrix (1999):** A hacker discovers reality is a simulated virtual world controlled by sentient machines, and he becomes part of the resistance.

2. **Ready Player One (2018):** In a dystopian future, people escape to the OASIS, a virtual reality universe. The movie follows a young hero on a quest to win control over this digital

realm.

3. **Tron (1982):** A computer programmer is transported into a digital world and must navigate his way through this dangerous and fascinating universe.

4. **eXistenZ (1999):** In a near-future where reality and virtual reality are blurred, a game designer on the run must play her latest virtual reality creation with a marketing trainee to determine if the game has been damaged.

5. **Inception (2010):** While not about VR in the traditional sense, this film explores the concept of entering and manipulating people's dreams, which parallels the immersive and manipulative nature of VR.

6. **The Lawnmower Man (1992):** A simple-minded gardener becomes the subject of a scientist's experiments in virtual reality and intelligence enhancement.

7. **Virtuosity (1995):** A virtual reality entity, which contains the personalities of multiple serial killers, escapes into the real world.

8. **Avatar (2009):** A paraplegic marine is dispatched to the moon Pandora on a unique mission and becomes torn between following his orders and protecting the world he feels is his home.

9. **Total Recall (1990/2012):** Both the original and the remake involve a protagonist who experiences a virtual reality memory implant that goes awry, blurring the lines between reality and simulation.

10. **Disclosure (1994):** This film features a virtual reality database, highlighting VR's potential in the corporate world.

11. **Brainstorm (1983):** Scientists invent a device that allows people to experience the sensations and emotions of others, blurring the lines between reality and virtual experience.

12. **Surrogates (2009):** People live their lives remotely from the safety of their homes via robotic surrogates—sexy, physically perfect mechanical representations of themselves.

13. **Strange Days (1995):** In a 1999 Los Angeles, a former cop turned street hustler accidentally uncovers a conspiracy in Los Angeles in 1999.

14. **Gamer (2009):** In a future where gamers control human beings in mass-scale, multiplayer online games, one star player from a game called "Slayers" looks to regain his independence.

15. **The Thirteenth Floor (1999):** In a virtual reality simulation of 1937, a man is suspected of murder. He discovers that his virtual world might be a key to the crime in the real world.

16. **Johnny Mnemonic (1995):** A data courier, carrying data package inside his mind, must deliver it before he dies from the overload or is killed by the Yakuza.

17. **.hack//SIGN (2002):** While not a movie, this anime series revolves around characters who are involved in a fictional MMORPG, and it dives deep into the world of VR gaming.

18. **Spy Kids 3: Game Over (2003):** The characters enter a virtual reality game to save their fellow spy kids.

19. **Black Mirror: Bandersnatch (2018):** A young programmer makes a fantasy novel into a game. The story becomes a dark adventure in the real world and in the game.

20. **VR.5 (1995):** Again, not a movie but a TV series that explored early concepts of virtual reality, where a woman discovers she can enter a virtual world using a dial-up modem and a headset.

These films range from science fiction to action and drama, each exploring different aspects and implications of virtual reality technology.

Augmented Reality (AR) and Extended Reality (XR)

Augmented Reality (AR) and Extended Reality (XR) are relatively newer concepts compared to Virtual Reality (VR), and as such, there are fewer movies directly focused on these themes. However, many films incorporate elements of AR, XR, or similar futuristic technologies that blend digital information with the physical world. Here's a list of 20 movies that touch on these themes or have elements akin to AR and XR:

1. **Minority Report (2002):** Features advanced AR interfaces, where Tom Cruise's character interacts with a computer with gesture-based controls.

2. **Iron Man (2008) and its sequels:** Tony Stark uses AR interfaces extensively, manipulating holographic data with his hands.

3. **Avatar (2009):** Showcases a form of XR where human consciousness is projected into alien bodies.

4. **Her (2013):** Focuses on AI and features elements of AR through immersive and interactive operating systems.

5. **Total Recall (1990/2012):** Both versions feature technologies that blend virtual experiences with real-life memories.

6. **The Terminator series:** The Terminator robots view the world with an overlay of data, akin to an AR perspective.

7. **RoboCop (1987/2014):** The RoboCop HUD (Heads-Up Display) provides real-time data, similar to AR.

8. **Star Wars series:** Holograms and interactive displays throughout the series resemble AR and XR technologies.

9. **Blade Runner (1982) and Blade Runner 2049 (2017):** Fea-

ture advanced technologies including holographic data and interactive interfaces.

10. **Prometheus (2012) and Alien: Covenant (2017):** Feature holographic mapping and interaction technologies.

11. **Mission Impossible series:** Uses various forms of futuristic tech, including AR-like gadgets and interfaces.

12. **Spy Kids 3: Game Over (2003):** Features a virtual game world, blending real and virtual elements.

13. **Back to the Future Part II (1989):** Features futuristic technologies including AR-like visors and glasses.

14. **Jumanji: Welcome to the Jungle (2017):** Players are drawn into a game world, blending real and digital experiences.

15. **Ready Player One (2018):** Although primarily VR-focused, it also includes elements where the virtual and physical worlds intersect.

16. **Wall-E (2008):** Features futuristic technology including holographic screens.

17. **The Fifth Element (1997):** Includes futuristic tech elements that are conceptually similar to AR.

18. **TRON: Legacy (2010):** The Grid is a digital world with real-world interactions, a concept extending towards XR.

19. **The Matrix series:** While it's more VR-centric, the idea of a digital reality overlaying the physical world aligns with XR concepts.

20. **Ender's Game (2013):** Features advanced interactive holographic interfaces and simulations.

These movies, while not always explicitly about AR or XR, showcase technologies and concepts that align closely with the principles of these realities – enhancing or extending the physical world with digital information and interaction.

Glossary

1. Augmented Reality (AR): A technology that overlays digital information (like images, text, or sound) onto the real-world environment.

2. Virtual Reality (VR): A simulated experience that can be similar to or completely different from the real world, typically involving visual and auditory immersion through a VR headset.

3. Extended Reality (XR): An umbrella term that covers Virtual Reality (VR), Augmented Reality (AR), and Mixed Reality (MR), encompassing all forms of combined real-and-virtual environments.

4. Mixed Reality (MR): A blend of physical and digital worlds, unlocking natural and intuitive interactions between humans, computers, and environment.

5. Head-Mounted Display (HMD): A device worn on the head that contains a display and lenses to view content in VR, AR, or MR.

6. 360-Degree Video: A video recording that captures every direction around the camera simultaneously, often used in VR environments.

7. Immersion: The sensation of being physically present in a non-physical world or the blending of the physical and virtual worlds in AR and MR.

8. Presence: The feeling of being in and interacting with a virtual environment or a digital overlay in AR.

9. Haptic Feedback: The use of touch (vibration or motion) to communicate with users, often used in VR controllers to enhance the sense of immersion.

10. Augmented Reality Markup Language (ARML): A standard used to specify and share AR experiences.

11. Eye Tracking: Technology that detects where a user is looking, often used in VR to enhance image rendering or in AR for interface interaction.

12. Gesture Recognition: The ability of a system to interpret human gestures and execute commands based on them, used in both AR and VR.

13. Field of View (FoV): The extent of the observable environment at any given moment, crucial in VR for immersion.

14. Latency: The delay between a user's action and the system's response, which is critical in VR and AR for maintaining immersion and avoiding motion sickness.

15. 6 Degrees of Freedom (6DoF): Refers to the freedom of movement in three-dimensional space, crucial for realistic movement in VR and MR environments.

16. Spatial Audio: Audio that changes based on the listener's position and orientation, enhancing realism in VR and AR.

17. Stereoscopic 3D: A technique for creating or enhancing the illusion of depth in an image by presenting two offset images separately to the left and right eyes.

18. Virtual Environment: A computer-generated setting in which users can interact, typical in VR.

19. AR Cloud: A persistent 3D digital copy of the real world to enable shared AR experiences across multiple devices.

20. Simultaneous Localization and Mapping (SLAM): A process used in AR and VR for mapping an environment and tracking the user's location within it.

21. Virtual Reality Modeling Language (VRML): A standard file format for representing 3D interactive vector graphics, designed particularly with the World Wide Web in mind.

22. Photogrammetry: The use of photography to measure and map environments, which can be used to create realistic 3D models for VR and AR.

23. Digital Twin: A virtual representation of a real-world entity or system, used in both AR and VR for simulations.

24. Telepresence: The use of VR or AR technology to feel present

in a location different from one's actual location.

25. Volumetric Capture: A technique of capturing an object in three dimensions, used for creating lifelike representations in VR and AR.

References

"Artificial Intelligence: A Guide for Thinking Humans" by Melanie Mitchell.

"Superintelligence: Paths, Dangers, Strategies" by Nick Bostrom.

"Virtual Reality" by Steven M. LaValle.

"The Fourth Transformation: How Augmented Reality & Artificial Intelligence Will Change Everything" by Robert Scoble and Shel Israel.

"Augmented Reality: Principles and Practice" by Dieter Schmalstieg and Tobias Höllerer.

"Artificial Intelligence: Foundations of Computational Agents" by David L. Poole and Alan K. Mackworth.

"Learning Virtual Reality: Developing Immersive Experiences and Applications for Desktop, Web, and Mobile" by Tony Parisi.

"Reality Check: How Immersive Technologies Can Transform Your Business" by Jeremy Dalton.

"Machine Learning Yearning" by Andrew Ng.

"Human Compatible: Artificial Intelligence and the Problem of Control" by Stuart Russell.

Google AI Blog: A resource for the latest news from Google on AI and machine learning research.

"The VR Book: Human-Centered Design for Virtual Reality" by Jason Jerald.

"Experience on Demand: What Virtual Reality Is, How It Works, and What It Can Do" by Jeremy Bailenson.

"Life 3.0: Being Human in the Age of Artificial Intelligence" by Max Tegmark.

"Introduction to Augmented Reality and Virtual Reality" by Jon Peddie.

MIT Technology Review: Provides articles and reports on the latest advancements in AI and VR.

"Handbook of Augmented Reality" edited by Borko Furht.

"Deep Learning" by Ian Goodfellow, Yoshua Bengio, and Aaron Courville.

"Augmented Reality: Where We Will All Live" by Jon Peddie.

VRScout.com: An online publication that covers the latest in VR and AR news and trends.

About the Author

John, with an illustrious career spanning over four decades in the Audio-Visual (AV) industry, has significantly contributed to various disciplines, including design, engineering, consulting, programming, integration, and manufacturing. He currently holds the position of Vice President of Engineering at PIVIUM, operating in both Meridian, Idaho, and Phoenix, Arizona. Additionally, John is the CEO of i-Create, LLC, a company specializing in digital arts and asset licensing.

As a thought leader in the AV space, John hosts "REALITY EXPANDED," a podcast available on SPOTIFY and APPLE PODCASTS

His extensive experience includes roles in AV product manufacturing and integration at Blonder Tongue and Smith Meeker Engineering from 1981 to 1986. He was a Partner and head of AV Consulting/Design with Shen Milsom & Wilke between 1987 and 1994 and served as a Principal at Cerami Associates from 1994 to 1996, where he initiated their AV Consulting/Design division.

John co-founded and led MDCI as CEO from 1996 to 2021, overseeing thousands of AV design engineering and programming projects. He also co-founded I-Create in 1996, focusing on IP intellectual properties, NFTs, and video games. His role as Director of Engineering, CAD, and Software Services at AVDG between 2018 and 2021 was pivotal in expanding the company's reach across Los Angeles, Chicago, Tennessee, and New Hampshire.

His historical project involvement includes over 6,000 completed projects in corporate, residential, educational, governmental, and military settings. John's expertise in the industry is further exemplified by his co-authorship of the InfoComm CTS-D course in 1996 and his sole authorship of its first re-write/update in 2006, earning him the AVIXA InfoComm Educator of the Year award for 2006.

As a Masters Certified Crestron programmer since 1988, John was the first third-party programmer for Crestron. His proficiency extends to various programming and design tools, including XCode, AutoCAD, Adobe Illustrator & Photoshop, DTools, and numerous graphic development programs. His professional certifications include CTS-D, CTS, Crestron Silver Masters, MTA-R, MSA-R, DMC-D, DMC-E, DMC-T, CTI, CSS-D, CSS-T, and CLC-C.

Fun Fact: John, a distinguished culinary professional and, along with his wife Dana, were the former co-owners of the Wine Spectator Award-winning "Pairings Wine Bar Restaurant" in Pleasanton, CA, has carved a niche in the culinary world with his exceptional skills and innovative approach. "Pairings Wine Bar Restaurant," known for its trendy and inviting ambiance, stood out in the local culinary scene under John's leadership.

The restaurant was celebrated for its eclectic and exclusive wine list, featuring selections from Old World, Napa, Lodi, Central Coast, and Livermore Valley wines. This specially curated list was designed to complement the restaurant's food offerings, enhancing the dining experience. Additionally, the establishment was known for offering 11 unique Private Label wines, further showcasing its commitment to providing a unique and refined selection for its patrons.

John's expertise extended to the culinary offerings at Pairings Wine Bar Restaurant, where the menu was characterized by a variety of small, shareable plates. These dishes were crafted to create an explosion of flavors on the palate, a testament to John's culinary prowess. The restaurant also boasted its own olive oils and balsamic vinegars, both used in its food items and featured in its tasting menu, adding a personal and artisanal touch to the dining experience.

Pairings Wine Bar Restaurant's excellence and uniqueness did not go unnoticed, as it was named one of the Top Ten Things To Do in the East Bay, a significant accolade highlighting its impact on the local food and wine scene.

John's background in culinary arts is rooted in his education from the prestigious Auguste Escoffier School of Culinary Arts, where he earned top honors in his class. His training at this renowned institution, coupled with his practical experience in the industry, has solidified his reputation as a culinary expert and innovative restaurateur.

www.ingramcontent.com/pod-product-compliance
Lightning Source LLC
Chambersburg PA
CBHW032026290526
45786CB00011B/526